THE WRITING ON THE
Chinese and Japanese immigration to B.C., ...

With tales of a gruesome murder, a typhoid epidemic, corrupt politicians, and a Japanese invasion, *The Writing on the Wall* was intended to shock its readers when it was published in 1921. Thinly disguised as a novel, it is a propaganda tract exhorting white British Columbians to greater vigilance to prevent greedy politicians from selling out to the Chinese and Japanese. It was also designed to convince eastern Canada of British Columbia's need for strict immigration regulations as protections against an onslaught of the 'yellow peril'.

This novel is not exceptional in its extreme racism; it reiterates almost every anti-oriental cliché circulating in British Columbia at the time of its publication. For example, the Chinese were repulsive individuals who lived in filth and indulged in illegal and immoral habits; the opium traffic threatened to undermine white society; the control of the vegetable market by the Chinese endangered the health of the white population. The Japanese were perceived as an even greater menace, systematically buying land to further Japan's imperialistic ambitions. While modern readers will find the story horrifying and unbelievable, it is in fact based on real incidents familar to the original audience.

In Canada the Oriental problem was unique to British Columbia but many of the views expressed on the west coast about Orientals were only exaggerated versions of ideas held elsewhere in the country about non-Anglo-Saxon immigrants. This novel is a vivid illustration of the fear and prejudice with which immigrants were regarded in the early twentieth century.

HILDA GLYNN-WARD was the literary pseudonym of Mrs Hilda G. Howard (1887–1966). Of Welsh birth, she came to Canada in 1910 and spent most of her life on southern Vancouver Island. She was a prolific writer of prose and poetry, and her best known work is *The Glamour of British Columbia*, a travel book published in 1926.

PATRICIA E. ROY is a member of the Department of History at the University of Victoria.

The illustration used first appeared on the jacket of the original edition published in Vancouver in 1921 by the Sun Publishing Company.

The writing on the wall

HILDA GLYNN-WARD

WITH AN INTRODUCTION BY PATRICIA E. ROY

UNIVERSITY OF TORONTO PRESS

© University of Toronto Press 1974

Reprinted in 2010

Toronto and Buffalo

Printed in Canada

ISBN 978-1-4426-1135-1 (paper)

Publication cataloguing information is available from Library and Archives Canada.

University of Toronto Press acknowledges the finanical assistance to its publishing program of the Canada Council for the Arts and the Ontario Arts Council.

University of Toronto Press acknowledges the financial support for its publishing activities of the Government of Canada through the Book Publishing Industry Development Program (BPIDP).

An introduction

BY PATRICIA E. ROY

Introduction

AS A WORK OF literature *The Writing on the Wall* is a penny dreadful. Like other examples of the genre, it was designed to shock readers, but it was also intended to educate rather than to entertain them. A reviewer declared that 'patriotism, not sensationalism, has inspired Mrs Glynn-Ward's book.' *The Writing on the Wall*, published in August 1921, is simply a propagandist tract. It sought to persuade white British Columbians to be vigilant lest greedy politicians sell them out to the Orientals and endeavoured 'to awaken those unbelievers in Eastern Canada who still wonder why the West is crying out on its knees for new immigration regulations.'[1] In Canada, although the Oriental problem was unique to British Columbia, many of the views expressed on the west coast about Orientals were exaggerated versions of ideas held elsewhere in the country about non-Anglo-Saxon immigrants.[2]

The novel's lack of literary sophistication contributes to its historical significance as an expression of the popular racist ideas circulating in British Columbia at the time of its publication. To most modern readers, *The Writing on the Wall* seems as pulpy as the paper on which the original edition was printed. However, many of its original readers in British Columbia undoubtedly took its message quite seriously, for they were being bombarded with propaganda describing the presence of Orientals in the province as a 'menace' to the future of white society.[3] Most of the incidents in the book seem to be the product of a hyperactive imagination; many, in fact, are based upon newspaper reports of actual events. Only in the concluding part of the novel does Mrs Glynn-Ward move into the realm of fantasy, but even in this horrific and seemingly preposterous depiction of the future she is not always original. Other publicists and politicians already had forecast many of the same terrors as the logical culmination of the Oriental penetration of British Columbia.

With its strong, crude, anti-Oriental bias, *The Writing on the Wall* fits into a long British Columbia tradition. A few examples of anti-Orientalism can be found as early as 1858, when the first permanent Chinese settlers arrived in Victoria as part of the flood of

Californians heading to the Fraser River gold fields. Before Confederation, however, anti-Oriental sentiment was expressed relatively infrequently. Then, in the late 1870s, provincial politicians took up the Chinese question.[4] Within the next decade, the legislature passed resolutions favouring restrictions on Chinese immigration, forbade their employment on public works, barred them from pre-empting or buying Crown land, and disenfranchised them. These were but the first of many legal disabilities imposed on the Chinese. Later, most of these restrictions were extended to the Japanese, many of whom began to arrive in the province in the 1890s. By 1921, Orientals in British Columbia were, with extremely rare exceptions, denied the municipal, provincial, and federal franchises and such related rights as eligibility for provincial or municipal elective office or employment and the opportunity to participate in such professions as law and pharmacy. The old legislation against their employment on public works contracts persisted and, in certain instances, they were denied employment on timber lands. Indeed, shortly before *The Writing on the Wall* appeared, the province had re-enacted the Oriental Orders In Council Validation Act relating to the employment of Orientals on timber lands. It is possible that Mrs Glynn-Ward is alluding to this act when she mentions a law passed 'two years ago' (p 19) to prevent Chinese from buying land from the government.[5]

The main thrust of British Columbia's long campaign against Orientals was directed at preventing their immigration rather than at regulating their activities after they had arrived. The concern about Chinese immigration which began in earnest in the late 1870s was stimulated in the 1880s as the CPR imported thousands of Chinese coolies to construct the railway through British Columbia. As much as the province wanted the railway, the legislature and British Columbia's members of parliament sought to have the railway employ white labour only.[6] However, neither the CPR nor the federal government was prepared to do so. In 1884, as the railway neared completion, British Columbia passed the first of many laws against Chinese immigration. This law was quickly disallowed by the federal government, which then appointed a royal commission to investigate. After the commission recommended the regulation of Chinese immigration rather than its complete cessation, British Columbia passed a Chinese Immigration Act identical to the one disallowed in

1884. The federal government again disallowed this legislation but did impose a fifty-dollar head tax on all Chinese entering Canada. This measure was quite ineffective.

By 1900, the legislature was regularly passing laws designed to prevent or discourage Oriental immigration. Most of these acts, however, were disallowed or rejected by the courts. In 1902, after yet another royal commission studied the question, the federal government raised the head tax to $500. Chinese immigration was briefly reduced, but, with a limited supply of Chinese labour and a booming economy, wages for Chinese soon rose and $500 ceased to be prohibitive.

During World War I, disruptions in trans-Pacific shipping and the serious unemployment situation in British Columbia which led the federal government to forbid the entry of unskilled alien labour to the province, sharply reduced Oriental, especially Chinese, immigration. This, however, was a temporary phenomenon. With the return of peace, many Chinese who had previously resided in Canada but who had spent the war years in China returned to British Columbia, as was their right under the 'registering out' or 'CI 9' clause of the Chinese Immigration Act. Since their return coincided with high unemployment and the return of soldiers to civilian life, the ensuing outburst of anti-Oriental sentiment was particularly strong.

In the meantime, the Oriental problem became more complicated as Japanese began to come to the province in large numbers. In 1907 a sudden, large influx of Japanese, Chinese, and East Indians aroused mobs who, incited to violence by the Asiatic Exclusion League, descended on the Chinese and Japanese sections of Vacouver, breaking windows and destroying merchandise.[7] After these riots, which attracted world-wide attention, the federal government negotiated the so-called Gentleman's Agreement, or Lemieux Agreement, under which Japan promised to restrict the number of emigrants to Canada. This secret agreement was ambiguous. British Columbians anticipated that only four hundred Japanese would be permitted to enter Canada each year; the Japanese government believed that the arrangement applied only to agricultural and domestic workers. Because of these conflicting interpretations, many British Columbians thought that Japan was not honouring her part of the bargain (p 42), whereas, in fact, she scrupulously followed it. In addition, many of the Japanese immigrants were 'picture' or mail order brides.

Thus the Oriental population of British Columbia, particularly the Japanese part of it, continued to increase. According to the 1911 census there were 19,568 Chinese and 8,587 Japanese in the province, which had a total population of 392,480. Ten years later, there were 23,532 Chinese and 15,006 Japanese in a total population of 542,582. Although the Chinese and Japanese formed less than one per cent of the Canadian population in 1921, they represented approximately seven per cent of British Columbia's population.

Opposition to the Oriental in British Columbia was general, but even rabid anti-Orientalists such as Mrs Glynn-Ward drew certain distinctions between the Chinese and the Japanese. The Chinese were repulsive individuals who lived in filth and indulged in illegal and immoral habits; the opium traffic threatened to undermine white society; their control of the vegetable market endangered the health of the white population. However, as Mrs Glynn-Ward clearly indicates, many British Columbians regarded the Japanese as a much greater menace than the Chinese to white society. The patient, persistent, and hard-working Japanese were eager to advance themselves, and bought up timber licences and mines, and 'were edging their way deep into the fish industry, they were even beginning to exploit their own natural industry, gardening...' (p 59). Unlike the Chinese, who usually resided in their own sections of the towns and countryside and whose conspiracies were the work of individuals rather than of the government of China, the Japanese bought land 'here and there and everywhere' (p 90), and in a pattern which xenophobes thought was related to the military and territorial ambitions of their mother country. The idea that the Japanese were 'double-crossers' (p 142) is indicative of the suspicions that white British Columbians felt about them. Moreover, as one of the characters in *The Writing on the Wall* observes, the Japanese 'are away cleverer and have more need of new colonies' (p 21).

Although many of the incidents in *The Writing on the Wall* appear fantastic to modern readers, they were based on true incidents which would have been familiar to British Columbians in 1921. The third part of the novel, 'The Future,' is purely imaginative, but contemporary readers would not have had to stretch their credulity to accept the plausibility of this scene as the consequence of the Oriental 'menace.'

By using actual place names, Mrs Glynn-Ward enhances the realism of the setting and increases the impact of her message. For example, in the opening scene, set in Vancouver in 1910, Point Grey Road, which parallelled the south shore of Burrard Inlet, was being settled as a new and fashionable residential district. The North Shore was expected to boom as soon as the Second Narrows Bridge was built; it was a good example of the real estate speculation gripping Vancouver at the time. (The bridge was not completed until 1925.)

The setting and mood ring true, but Mrs Glynn-Ward makes no attempt to be historically precise.[8] Style-conscious women might very well have shopped at Drysdale's in 1910, but they would have found only one Chinese and one Japanese store on Granville Street, a major shopping artery, and both of them were Oriental curio shops not directly competing with local merchants. By 1921, however, there were at least three Japanese dry goods stores on this street. At that time, retail merchants were vigorously complaining about Oriental competition, although most of the Chinese and Japanese stores were small groceries and confectioneries. Fort Edward is probably the name for Port Edward, a community nine miles from Prince Rupert. Although there were copper mines on the north coast, the Fort Edward mines were imaginary and the fish cannery, the main industry of Port Edward, was not opened until 1913. The murder in 1910 of Mrs Smith by Sam Wong was based on an actual event, the death in 1914 of Mrs. C.J. Millard, the wife of a CPR official, at the hands of Jack Kong, her Chinese schoolboy servant. The murder and Kong's trial — as the novel records he was found guilty of manslaughter — were reported in newspapers in all their grisly particulars and caused as much excitement throughout British Columbia as the murder in the novel. The original readers of the novel, though familiar with many of the events recounted, probably only vaguely recalled that they took place before the war.

One of the advertisements for *The Writing on the Wall* suggested that readers could recognize the characters of the book.[9] This was misleading. Mrs Glynn-Ward was too clever to risk any possibility of a libel suit. It is impossible to identify any of her main characters precisely with any real person. Only Carter McRobbie was vaguely

drawn from life. His interest in fish canning may have been based on
that of Harlan C. Brewster, premier of British Columbia from the
1916 Liberal victory to his death in March 1918. Brewster was a fish
canner but, unlike McRobbie, he was reported to have boasted of
operating his canneries without the use of Chinese labour. Moreover,
he was not a wealthy man. There is a closer parallel between
McRobbie and James Dunsmuir, lieutenant-governor from 1906 to
1909. Dunsmuir's family had founded a coal-mining empire on Vancouver Island which depended to a large extent on the use of cheap
Oriental labour. In 1907, Dunsmuir reserved[10] one of the Natal Acts
or language tests which the legislature passed regularly between 1900
and 1908 in an attempt to curb the flow of Oriental immigrants to
the province. (The other acts were disallowed by the federal government.) The fact that Dunsmuir, a major employer of Oriental labour,
reserved the bill aroused great protest, especially among organized
labour which, a few months later, participated in burning him in
effigy as a prelude to the infamous parade which led to the anti-
Asiatic riots in Vancouver. McRobbie is remarkably like Dunsmuir in
his desire to have cheap labour, but in the dénouement of the novel,
he is the very antithesis of Dunsmuir.

The notion that provincial politicians were corrupt was common-
place in British Columbia in 1921. During the previous decade there
had been many allegations about the alienation of natural resources
by large corporations, and about cabinet ministers using their
positions for personal benefit and accepting campaign funds from
contractors beholden to the government. In 1916 such charges contributed to the defeat of the Conservatives, who had governed the
province since 1903. The victorious Liberals quickly investigated the
more serious charges, particularly those relating to the construction
of the Pacific Great Eastern Railway. A select committee of the
legislature heard testimony that the company, a generous con-
tributor to Conservative party funds, had concluded an illegal contract with the provincial government, but the committee had
insufficient evidence to pursue the matter into the courts.

While the Liberals cast stones at the Conservatives, they were not
themselves innocent of wrongdoing. The attorney-general resigned
after an investigation of charges that 'pluggers' had voted for him in
a Vancouver by-election. The administration of prohibition created
embarrassment when the prohibition commissioner pleaded guilty to

importing and selling whisky on his own behalf. Even 'Honest' John Oliver, who had succeeded to the premiership in March 1918, was not above suspicion. He was accused of using his position to obtain, for his personal benefit, land which should have gone to the Soldiers' Settlement Board. The premier successfully sued his accuser for libel, but was awarded only twenty-five cents in damages. Although the jury ruled that the effect on his reputation had been negligible, the suspicion that all was not well within the government lingered. Indeed, the supposedly Liberal Vancouver *Sun* assailed the provincial administration for its crooked deals and for being subservient to the 'big interests' of the province. Several defeated Liberal candidates in the federal election of 1921 attributed their failure to the defection of many Liberals who were disgusted with the local party.

In this context, British Columbians were not required to exercise much imagination to conclude that 'the skids might be greased' for such acts as the illegal importation of opium (p 25) or immigrants (pp 42, 71). Mrs Glynn-Ward based her stories of opium smuggling and illegal immigration on widespread rumours. For example, in 1910, reports circulated in Vancouver that customs officers, civic officials, and even William Templeman, a federal cabinet minister, had participated in schemes to smuggle Chinese labourers into Canada. After examining the matter for the federal government, Mr Justice Murphy concluded that ample opportunities for such an operation existed at Vancouver and some Vancouver Island ports but not at Victoria. He also determined that a few Chinese and some minor officials in the customs service had participated in frauds but he cleared Templeman and civic officials of all charges.

In *The Writing on the Wall,* the politicians were unusually silent on the Oriental question. At no point does Morley or any of his associates make a public statement against Oriental competition or immigration. In real life, politicians regularly denounced the Oriental presence and, in election platforms, promised to restrict Oriental activities and to halt Oriental immigration. Only among the Socialists could be found politicians who did not have anti-Oriental statements on their records.

Traditionally, organized labour had been in the vanguard of critics of Oriental immigration. Workingmen saw the Oriental with his low standard of living as an unfair competitor who was willing to work long hours for low wages and under conditions, including strike-breaking, intolerable to white men. In certain cases, particularly in the coal mines, the presence of Orientals was alleged to be dangerous to the safety of all workers.

As early as 1878, a general union, the Workingman's Protective Association, was organized in Victoria to protect the working class of the province against the Chinese influx. Although this association lasted briefly, opposition to Oriental labour had been declared a policy of the labour movement. Twelve years later, in 1890, British Columbia delegates to the Trades and Labour Congress convention vigorously pressed a resolution for Chinese exclusion. The passage of such a resolution became virtually an annual event at Congress conventions.

By 1919, however, the increasing strength of international socialism within the provincial labour movement led the BC Federation of Labour to drop its anti-Oriental stance. Nevertheless, several members of the Vancouver Trades and Labour Council were prominent in the Asiatic Exclusion League, which was founded in Vancouver in 1921 (see p xxiii). Labour had not completely abandoned Oriental exclusion; indeed, it was one of the issues which contributed to the disunity of the labour movement during the 1920s.[11] Because of this disunity, labour ceased to be an important factor in stimulating anti-Oriental sentiment in that decade. When the *BC Federationist,* then the mouthpiece of radical elements in the labour movement, reviewed *The Writing on the Wall* — almost six months after its publication — the novel was described as merely 'a chain of incidents which serve as pegs on which to hang tit-bits of racial jealousy.'[12]

This comment is a little surprising. Mrs Glynn-Ward uses the traditional argument of labour and the socialists that capitalists had imported cheap Oriental labour in a selfish endeavour to increase their own profits. The point of her argument is that greedy capitalists and corrupt politicians had sold the province to the Orientals. Thus, Carter McRobbie, the fish canner, and Gordon Morley, the entrepreneur and politician, become major villains. In fact, Morley is an arch-villain. He is painted as a selfish individual who knows 'no other gods but himself' (p 6) and his snobbish, social-climbing wife is no more likeable. Morley induces unsuspecting individuals to invest in North Shore land when he knows the Second Narrows Bridge is unlikely to be built; he accepts campaign funds from Chinese in return for promises to build certain roads; and, with Craddock Low, his lawyer friend, he even exploits McRobbie. In this exploitation he commits one of his vilest acts, the appointment of a Chinese collaborator to the post of assistant controller of customs at Victoria. In return, Morley receives assistance in evading the head tax on Chinese labour imported for his own lumber mills and for McRobbie's cannery. After describing this last incident, Mrs Glynn-Ward states her main thesis:

The foundations for the sale of British Columbia into the hands of the Orientals were laid — by Politicians whose sole aim was self-glorification, power, money; little souls with brains top-heavy with cunning, using their country and their fellows as stepping-stones to notoriety and a big bank account; by Capitalists who exploited the riches of their country and the necessities of the people in order that they themselves might profit, and live in ease and luxury, who denying all the responsibilities of wealth and power lived merely by the rule of Devil-take-the-hindmost; by every citizen who shut his eyes rather than see what he didn't wish to see, who, like the ostrich buried his head in the sand rather than face unpleasant truths and take a stand against them. [p 73]

In the conclusion, Mrs Glynn-Ward underlines this theme by having McRobbie and a fellow MLA agree that because of their personal pecuniary interests in enterprises which depended on cheap Oriental labour they have had to do the bidding of Chinese and Japanese bosses and accept the enfranchisement of Oriental landowners — the ultimate step in the downfall of a white British Columbia.

It is only late in *The Writing on the Wall* that any reference is made to the Oriental franchise. Its inclusion as a signal of the beginning of the end of 'British' Columbia again reflects contemporary popular ideas. In 1920, by a single vote, the legislature defeated a bill to enfranchise those residents of Japanese origin who were Canadian citizens or British subjects and who had served in the Canadian Expeditionary Force during the war. One of the main arguments against this proposal, which would have affected fewer than 150 people, was that it was the 'thin edge of the wedge,' an argument which Mrs Glynn-Ward puts into McRobbie's mouth as he debates with himself the signing of a bill to enfranchise Oriental landowners (p 112).

The question of Oriental ownership of land was a live one in the 1920s, as it had been before the war. Chinese had been engaged in market gardening near Vancouver and Victoria for many years, but they usually leased their land, possibly because they could not buy or pre-empt Crown land. During the war, Orientals, especially Japanese in the Fraser Valley, had increased their land holdings, partly through the 'block-busting' techniques described in the novel (p 90). In the Okanagan there were rumours of large land purchases by the Japanese. However, Mrs Glynn-Ward makes only passing mention of this area, where the fear of an Oriental takeover was great, and she refers only to the Chinese who had large gardens in the northern part of the valley. In 1919 and 1920, boards of trade and agricultural organizations such as the Farmers' Institutes and the BC Fruit Growers' Association passed resolutions against the owning or leasing of land by Orientals. In several areas, farmers voluntarily agreed not to sell or lease land to Orientals. Thus, one of the few heroes in *The Writing on the Wall* is Robert Laidlaw, who adamantly refuses to sell out to the Chinese.

Because of international complications, particularly relating to the Japanese, the British Columbia government refused to legislate against the sale or leasing of land to Orientals. Nevertheless, it did collect statistical data on the extent of Oriental land holding and used this information to bolster its case for the abrogation of the Anglo-Japanese Treaty of Commerce and Navigation. Figures published in June 1921 revealed that slightly over 1,000 Chinese and Japanese owned or leased 27,000 acres of land in British Columbia.[13] This was not a large amount of land, but it was concentrated in a few parts of the province and was intensively cultivated.

In addition, Oriental farmers were successful competitors. The novel's portrayal of a situation in which the Chinese monopolized the fresh vegetable industry seems exaggerated, but in the summer of 1921 the provincial department of agriculture reported that ninety per cent of the produce supplied to the city markets of Vancouver and fifty-five per cent of the potatoes grown in the province were raised by Chinese farmers.[14] The Chinese were also prominent in the distribution of fruit and vegetables. The Chinese pedlar going from door to door with his baskets of fresh produce was a familiar sight on city streets. Retail grocers complained of these competitors and of the Chinese greengrocers who kept long hours, displayed their wares attractively, and sold general grocery items as well as perishables. Through the imposition of heavy licence fees and the enforcement of by-laws relating to shop-closing hours, the cities and municipalities tried to remove some of the competitive advantages of the Chinese merchants. The white shopkeepers, however, could not overcome a basic problem. As the novel suggests (p 9), white housewives often preferred the Chinese stores, which offered better service and prices. In the final section of the novel the white population is dying from typhoid fever transmitted by Chiense-grown vegetables and sugar packed by Chinese who deliberately added typhoid germs to it. The Chinese and Japanese, however, remain healthy since they have been 'innured to it by countless generations of living without sanitation' (p 132). This horrific scene is one of the best examples of Mrs Glynn-Ward's attempt to convince British Columbians of the evils of patronizing Oriental merchants.

In urging consumers to avoid eating vegetables grown by Chinese who used human waste as fertilizer, Mrs Glynn-Ward was repeating a variation of the old belief that the Chinese handled food unsanitarily.[15] Another version of this belief was the advertisement of the BC Sugar Refining Company in the spring of 1914 that Hong Kong sugar was 'refined by semi-naked, unwashed, steaming, smelly coolies [and] has a fine chance to become inoculated with all the unpleasant things which such conditions are likely to produce.' In 1920, the legislature's select standing committee on agriculture recommended that the department of health investigate reports that Orientals were not observing the sanitary laws of the province.[16] The notion that Chinese might deliberately contaminate the food supply (p 133) would not have seemed completely absurd to naive readers in 1921.

It was difficult for the province to do anything about the Chinese who were already on the land. In the long run, a far greater worry was the apparently systematic acquisition of land by the Japanese.

Despite disclaimers by the Japanese consul, it was widely believed that the Japanese government made low interest loans to its subjects to buy land in British Columbia (p 59). *The Writing on the Wall,* repeatedly suggests that these purchases were related to Japan's imperial ambitions. Japanese immigrants bought land at strategic locations such as the north side of the Fraser River (pp 59, 92, 95) and the Queen Charlotte Islands (p 55). Japanese fishermen possessed elaborate maps and charts of the coast (p 61). The sinister possibilities of the facts are demonstrated in the concluding scene when the Japanese use these sites and their knowledge of the region to launch a surprise attack on the province.

That Japan should be seen as a military threat in the early 1920s seems strange since Japan had been allied to Britain and hence Canada since 1902. Nevertheless, Mrs Glynn-Ward was not alone in finding evidence of Japan's military ambitions. Fifteen years earlier, the idea of Japan as a military threat had been an essential part of the campaign of William Hearst, the American newspaper publisher, against the 'yellow peril.' More recently, missionaries and other visitors from the Orient had warned British Columbia audiences of Japan's military ambitions.[17] A few weeks after the publication of *The Writing on the Wall,* the Penticton *Herald* observed that the Japanese invariably preferred land as close to the United States border as possible, that many Japanese males in Canada had done military service in Japan, and that most of the Japanese women in British Columbia were of child-bearing age. The *Herald* concluded that 'one does not have to be an alarmist to see here some palpable proof of an Asiatic menace.' Two Vancouver Island newspapers reprinted the editorial.[18]

Of immediate concern to British Columbia was the matter of illegal immigration. As the novel suggests, this took several forms. One was the exploitation of loopholes in the immigration law and its administration (p 104). The $500 head tax was not an effective deterrent because Canadian corporations desiring cheap labour arranged with Chinese agents in British Columbia to advance travel costs and the head tax to immigrant labourers.[19] When *The Writing on the Wall* appeared, labourers were not being admitted, but many Chinese were legally returning to Canada after 'registering out' for lengthy visits to their native land.

The Chinese Immigration Act also made provision for the entry of 'students' and 'merchants.' The former were required to deposit $500 when they arrived in Canada, but this sum was refunded when they left. 'Merchants' and their families were admitted free. There were abuses on a large scale. When labourers were not being admitted, the number of Chinese 'students' increased but the department of immigration 'found most of them in laundries.'[20] The abuse of the 'merchant' class was much greater. Canada had understood 'merchant' to mean an individual of substantial means engaged in the import-export trade who would return to his native land once his business was accomplished. Since Canada lacked her own consular officials in China she relied on the British foreign service which, in turn, relied on the Chinese commissioner of foreign affairs to investigate the status of would-be immigrants and to certify them as 'merchants.' A Canadian immigration official who visited China early in 1921 found that the Chinese commissioner was certifying many small shopkeepers and store clerks. The Canadian official reported that Chinese with connections in Vancouver made all the arrangements for these 'merchant' immigrants including their passage, their documentation, and the payment of necessary 'squeeze money' (bribes) in China.[21] To counteract this abuse of the act, the Canadian government abolished certification for merchants and required 'every Chinese merchant landing on our western coasts to satisfy the controller of immigration there as to the bonafides of his status.'[22]

One of the critical incidents in *The Writing on the Wall* is the appointment of a Chinese as assistant controller of customs at Victoria with responsibility for registering the names of all Chinese entering Canada (p 73). In fact, this was a federal and not, as the novel implies, a provincial post. Nevertheless, there is some substance for Mrs Glynn-Ward's story. The senior officials in charge of controlling Chinese immigration were whites, but they depended on Chinese interpreters. In 1920, H.H. Stevens, Conservative MP for Vancouver Centre, alleged that there had been corruption involving the Chinese interpreter at Vancouver. The charges could not be substantiated and immigration officials concluded that there had been a deliberate frame-up but misgivings remained in the public mind. In a sense, this suspicion was later confirmed. In 1931, the immigration department discovered that because of lax and inefficient enforcement of its regulations and the malfeasance of some employees, particularly a Japanese interpreter, approximately 2,500 Japanese had entered Canada illegally since 1923.[23]

Mrs Glynn-Ward also suggests that many Japanese entered the country surreptitiously via sampans which crossed the Pacific and landed their human cargoes at isolated points on the coast. Imaginative as this episode seems, for sampans are very small boats, it had some inspiration in fact. In 1913, nine Japanese were apprehended at Bella Bella after having been brought by junk from Japan in an attempt to enter the United States illegally. The would-be immigrants were deported and the junk disappeared.[24] This notion of illegal Japanese immigration became part of the anti-Japanese mythology of the province. In 1938, to allay the worries of some British Columbians, the federal government appointed a special board to investigate rumours of illegal Japanese immigration including the landing of Japanese at isolated coastal points. The board could not verify these reports and found that the closer it got to the scene of the supposed landing places, the less the local residents knew about it.

In describing the use of illegal fishing methods by the Japanese and the desire of the canners for more fishermen, Mrs Glynn-Ward again deals with a very real situation. At a fisheries inquiry held in the fall of 1919, witnesses charged that the seines and traps used by Japanese fishermen off Vancouver Island were responsible for the depletion of the fisheries.[25] This, however, was only one part of the complaint against Japanese fishermen who, in 1919, held almost half the commercial fishing licenses issued in the province. Most of the rhetoric against the Japanese was directed at the need to keep the fisheries for white men rather than at the need to preserve a natural resource. Consequently, the federal government adopted an 'open door' policy whereby it granted an unlimited number of licences to white and native Indian British subjects while freezing at the 1919 level the number of gill net licences to other nationalities. This policy reduced the proportion of Japanese in the fisheries without antagonizing the canners who wanted more fishermen.

The opposition to the Oriental was not wholly economic. The racial prejudice underlying many of the efforts to preserve a white British Columbia is clearly expressed in *The Writing on the Wall* in the derogatory terms 'Chink,' 'Jap,' 'yellow devil' and 'little brown men,' and in the stereotypes about the Oriental which are applied to individuals as well as to the group. Chung Lee, the Chinese conspirator, has difficulty in pronouncing English words such as 'wunyuns' (onions) and 'callatee' (carrots). He waits 'stoically, as those of the East wait, with never a shadow of an expression on his thick and stolid face and never an extra gleam of expectancy in his narrow little pig eyes' (p 23). The police chief refers to him as 'the wiliest fish' that the force has dealt with particularly since 'if you look for one Chung Lee, you can find a dozen of the same name, and they're all so blamed alike' (p 25). Yet, despite her repetition of the traditional descriptions of the Chinese, Mrs Glynn-Ward is an alert observer. The Chinese in the 1910 scene are 'pig-tailed'; in 1920 they are not (p 77). In describing the Chinese collectively, she also uses stereotypes to paint a dismal picture of their society. The only Chinese residences in the novel are opium dens whose floors are 'littered with filth indescribable, and [where] the stench of cesspools rose to meet the soul-killing fumes of opium' (p 33). When the Chinese are not lying in a drug-induced torpor, they are engaged in the other traditional Chinese vice — gambling.

In 1921, there was a nation-wide campaign in progress against the illegal drug traffic. This took several forms, including a series of articles by Judge Emily Murphy of Edmonton in *Maclean's Magazine*, newspaper articles and editorials and the formation, in Vancouver, of a White Cross Society to combat the drug menace. When H.H. Stevens told parliament that the drug traffic was 'not *wholly* attributable to Asiatics yet the basis of traffic is Asiatic,'[26] he reflected public opinion in British Columbia. Except for the sensationalist press in Vancouver, the agitation against the drug trade was not exclusively directed against the Chinese. Nevertheless, had Mrs Glynn-Ward wanted more lurid examples of the Oriental influence on the drug trade she could have found tales of young whites falling into evil ways as a result of exposure to drugs in Chinatown. Significantly, the only non-Oriental addict in *The Writing on the Wall* is the lawyer, Craddock Low, who, with Morley, becomes involved in the traffic for reasons of greed.

The novel, of course, does not ignore the fear that close contact with Orientals endangered the morals of young whites. There is a whole chapter describing the horrors of the elopement and disappearance, presumably into white slavery, of a young white woman of good family who has been wooed by a former Chinese schoolmate. Ironically, the girl's father has aided Morley in his opium-smuggling activities. The fear that Oriental children were a corrupting influence in the schools was a real one. Within a few months of the publication of *The Writing on the Wall* there was a debate in Vancouver on the effects on the morals and health of white children by the presence of Oriental children in the same classroom. The discussion was provoked by specific incidents: the publication of statistics showing that the number of Oriental children was increasing four times as rapidly as the white student population; the presence of over-age immigrants in elementary classes; and the outbreak of a minor diphtheria epidemic after a Japanese child contracted the disease. Although the Vancouver school board observed an increase in prejudice against Oriental school children, it did not consider the establishment of segregated schools to be practical. In Victoria, however, the school board undertook such a programme during the 1922-3 school year but abandoned it after the Chinese boycotted the segregated school and the Chinese consul intervened on their behalf.

School board officials justified the segregated school by arguing that Oriental children, with an inadequate knowledge of English, retarded the academic progress of their white classmates. Not all principals who had Oriental children in their schools agreed that this was so. Published school examination results indicated that some Oriental children were excellent scholars. One of the characters in the novel complains: 'they're cleverer than us ... specially the Japs, you'll see them at the top o' the class and the white kids at the bottom every time!' (p 85). This remark, of course, reflects a major reason for concern about the Oriental, the fear that by their ability and hard work they would take over the province.

The school question also revealed the fear that familiarity between Oriental and white children might lead to intermarriage. Inassimilability is a constant theme in the rhetoric of anti-Orientalism and was given additional stimulus in the early 1920s by such Americans as Madison Grant, author of *The Passing of the Great Race* (1916), and Lothrop Stoddard, who in 1920 published *The Rising Tide of Color Against White World-Supremacy*. In the latter book, which included references to the Oriental question in British

Columbia, Stoddard declared that there was 'a very imminent danger
that the white stock may be swamped by Asiatic blood.' He also
warned that races followed Gresham's Law, namely that bad blood
drove out good.[27] Stoddard's ideas were publicized in British
Columbia; he was quoted by name and his views endorsed in such
diverse sources as political speeches and the medical advice column
of a daily newspaper. It is also quite likely that J.S. Cowper, a
former maverick Liberal MLA, was inspired by Stoddard to entitle
his series of newspaper articles in *The Vancouver World* 'The Rising
Tide of Asiatics.'

British Columbians, however, did not need American writers to
inform them of impending dangers to the white race. For example,
in 1919, H.H. Stevens told a meeting sponsored by the Missionary
Society of Mount Pleasant Methodist Church that the Asiatic
question was 'simply one of the preservation of racial type. ... The
question is ... one of assimilation, and putting it bluntly, assimilation
after all means intermarriage. ... The Asiatic will never make a good
citizen. He may be intelligent, he may be fully educated to Canadian
customs and standards, and he may be an asset to Canada in the way
of production; but the barrier of race is insurmountable, and he will
never be assimilated.' Five years earlier, the Vancouver *Sun* had
commented on the 'instinctive repugnance among the white races to
marriage with Orientals. ... All experience goes to show that it would
take generations to break down the social and family barriers
between the Japs and the Chinese and the whites, if indeed it could
ever be effected. ... If British Columbia is to be a white man's
country, the whites must have a fair chance. ... It is a matter of race
preservation... '[28] Thus it is not surprising that a character in *The
Writing on the Wall* asserts: 'This is a white man's country. We can't
mix with them – that is, they can't become Canadians... ' (p 55).
Equally reminiscent of contemporary racial rhetoric is Morley's
explanation of the horrors of the concluding scene as the consequence of meddling 'with Nature in our attempt to mix East with
West ... ' (p 146).

Although anti-Orientalism and Oriental stereotypes have appeared
in other British Columbia novels, they have never been more than
incidental themes.[29] *The Writing on the Wall* is therefore the only

specifically anti-Oriental novel published in the province. But is only in form that the book is unique; its ideas were being conveyed to British Columbians by a variety of means. In the summer of 1921 an anti-Oriental campaign, which peaked with the federal election of December 1921 and culminated with the passage of the Chinese Immigration Act in 1923, was launched. The publicity for this campaign began in mid-July with the publication of the first of the series of columns by J.S. Cowper. In these articles, Cowper described the increasing penetration of Orientals into the economy of the province. Much of what he said was similar to the message of *The Writing on the Wall.* Indeed, Cowper made a vague claim to having inspired the novel.[30] The *World* was not alone in calling for restrictions on Oriental immigration. During 1921 at least one and frequently many editorials on the subject appeared in almost every British Columbia daily and weekly newspaper.

The chief agency for promoting anti-Oriental sentiment, the Asiatic Exclusion League, had been founded by several trade union leaders, representatives of returned soldiers organizations and the Retail Merchants Association. The league hired canvassers, provided speakers for any group which would sponsor them, and soon claimed to have 20,000 members and branches in several provincial centres. Mrs Glynn-Ward was elected to the executive of the group in early September but her name does not appear in the list of officers after a reorganization in late October. By that time a rival, but anonymous group, the Danger Publishing Company, was producing *Danger: The Anti-Asiatic Weekly.* This journal warned against Japan's military ambitions, the illegal drug traffic, and the enfranchisement of Orientals. It also criticized the promotional methods of the Asiatic Exclusion League. Since Mrs Glynn-Ward wrote for *Danger* and her book was advertised as being available for $1.30 through the publishing company, it is possible that her withdrawal from the league was linked to the competition between the two anti-Oriental groups. The evidence, however, is so scanty that only conjecture is possible.

The anti-Oriental agitation, designed not only to arouse British Columbians but also to impress eastern Canadians, had some concrete results. In 1923 the federal government passed a new Chinese Immigration Act which effectively ended Chinese immigration by limiting entry to such Chinese as diplomats, international traders, and students who, by the nature of their callings, would not be remaining permanently in Canada. In the same year, Canada secured a modification in the Gentleman's Agreement whereby Japan reduced from four hundred to one hundred and fifty the number of agricultural and domestic workers permitted to enter Canada annually. Five years later, after extensive diplomatic negotiations, Japan agreed to restrict the total number of immigrants to Canada to one hundred and fifty per year and to end the custom of Canadian Japanese sending home for 'picture brides.'[31]

Because of the extent and variety of anti-Oriental agitation in the early 1920s, it is impossible to isolate the impact of *The Writing on the Wall*. The record of specific reaction to it is slim. Book reviews were not a feature of most British Columbia newspapers. The Vancouver *Sun,* which published the novel, was one of the few journals to have a regular book column. It gave *The Writing on the Wall* brief but favourable mention — two months after publication. On the other hand, the *British Columbia United Farmer* reviewed it promptly and enthusiastically, declaring that 'the story will bring home to readers in a striking manner the real dangers of the situation.'[32] Politically, there is no evidence of the novel being specifically mentioned on the hustings, but when the new parliament met in 1922, A.W. Neill (Independent, Comox-Alberni) told the Commons that he had asked the parliamentary librarian to purchase half a dozen copies of *The Handwriting on the Wall* [sic], 'a book of truth dealing with the Asiatic question, particularly the Japanese phase of it, on our coast to-day.'[33] The Chinese community also felt the novel's effects. Reminiscing about anti-Oriental sentiment, Foon Sien, a prominent Vancouver Chinese, declared in 1949 that Mrs Glynn-Ward was 'selling hatred to the innocent public. ... '[34]

Little is known about Mrs Glynn-Ward herself. The name was a pseudonym; in real life she was Mrs Hilda G. Howard. The daughter of a classical scholar, W. Glynn Williams, she was born in 1887 in Wales, where she was also educated. Before coming to Canada in 1910 she travelled extensively. In 1920, while living in Vancouver, she turned to free-lance journalism, but the first record of her appearing as a public personality in British Columbia is in April 1921, when she spoke to the provincial retail grocers' convention in

Vancouver on the subject of Chinese immigration. Her speech on that occasion was a forecast of many of the arguments of *The Writing on the Wall.*[35]

After publishing her novel in 1921, Mrs Glynn-Ward continued to be convinced of the danger posed by the presence of Orientals. In the preface to a travel book published in 1926 she refers to 'the little Jap who, laughing up and down his sleeve, goes cheerfully about his business in a gas-boat up the coast, or picks out the best small-fruit land in the country; the ubiquitous Chinaman, steadily cornering all the loose cash in the land – of a surety these two know more of British Columbia than most white men![36] Anti-Oriental sentiment also appears in her poetry, as when, in 'Many Types – Being Reflections at the Empress Hotel' she describes:

Japanese bell-boys, slick and stealthy
Pocketing tips that make them wealthy.[37]

She was also an inveterate writer of letters to the editor. Over the years, her letters covered such diverse topics as the efficiency of the provincial police in catching rum runners; the lack of government measures to control cougars, bears, and stray dogs; the development of hydro-electric power on the Columbia River and the advantages of Social Credit's 'pay as you go' policies. In 1942 she began writing letters on the need for fair and just treatment of native Indians. Despite her hatred of the Orientals, she could sympathize with the problems of another race. To readers of *The Writing on the Wall,* this is not really surprising. In it the Indians are stereotyped as lazy and unreliable (p 19). Thus they posed no threat to the status quo of white society. Mrs Glynn-Ward could easily afford to be paternalistic towards the Indians and simultaneously use their maltreatment to criticize the government.

The sincerity of her fears about the Oriental as expressed in *The Writing on the Wall* is demonstrated by the consistency of her argument of the years. Although her address changed – California, Kamloops, and various points in and near Victoria – she always signed her anti-Oriental letters as 'H. Glynn-Ward, Author of "The Writing on the Wall" .' Included in these letters were references to illegal immigration, the dangers of intermarriage, and the need to keep British Columbia a white man's country. In 1935, when members of the CCF proposed to enfranchise the Orientals, she warned that giving the vote to 40,000 Orientals would mean

in no time at all ... a preponderance of Orientals in the local legislature. And do those who are going to vote for the CCF realize that they would have a mighty poor chance of direct or indirect government jobs with, for instance, a Japanese minister of public works?

The basic fault lies with the iniquitous kind of party politics that is the curse of Canada and has been the ruin of this province. Had we even a fairly good government free of party graft and corruption there would have been no reason for the existence of the CCF or any other body with traitorous, anti-British intentions. The time is ripe for all loyal, politics-weary British Columbians to rise up and petition No. 10, Downing Street to take over the government of this province as it did that of Newfoundland [in 1933] with such beneficial results.[38]

Mrs Glynn-Ward had revived the themes of *The Writing on the Wall* with full vigour. Her suggestion that British Columbia return to colonial status may have been mere hyperbole but readers of the novel will note that one of the tragic incidents in the concluding scene is the withdrawal of 'Columbia' from the British Empire and the establishment of a 'Republic of Canada,' which cannot 'ask or expect help from her erstwhile Mother – England' (p 142).

After Japan attacked Pearl Harbor, three weeks passed before a letter from Mrs Glynn-Ward appeared in the press. She refrained from indulging herself in the partial vindication of her twenty-year-old predictions. Instead, she was more concerned about the immediate situation. She blamed the reluctance of the federal government to protect the province from the 30,000 Japanese within it on the presence of fifth columnists in Ottawa.[39] Although this notion of fifth columnists was a bit extreme and paranoid even by contemporary British Columbia standards, it typified popular opinion in the province about the danger posed by the Japanese within it. Indeed, while the major newspapers counselled British Columbians to remain calm, politicians, public organizations, and individuals deluged the federal government with demands to intern the Japanese or remove them from the coast. Late in February 1942, Ottawa, yielding to this apparent hysteria, ordered all persons of Japanese descent, including natives of Canada, to leave the coastal region.

After the war, Mrs Glynn-Ward continued to believe in the impossibility of assimilation. If anything, her views on the subject were stronger than before. 'The Almighty,' she asserted, 'designed the different races of man and set them on different continents so that there shold be no freak off-spring.' As 'a most Christian act,' she proposed that the Japanese be returned 'carriage paid as speedily as possible to their own country.'[40] Many British Columbians also favoured the repatriation of all Japanese, including those who were Canadian-born. In 1947, however, Ottawa abandoned its plans to deport Japanese who did not wish to go to Japan.

The day of the rampant anti-Oriental sentiment in British Columbia that had permitted the circulation of such propaganda as *The Writing on the Wall* and had led to the evacuation of the Japanese from the coast in 1942 was rapidly disappearing. Despite Pearl Harbor, the nightmare Mrs Glynn-Ward predicted did not come to pass. Instead, Japan had been defeated, China was weak. Within British Columbia the Orientals were no longer the obvious 'menace' they once had been. The Japanese had been dispersed across the country; without immigration, the predominantly male Chinese population had declined. Whereas in 1921 Orientals had accounted for approximately one in every fourteen British Columbians, by 1951 their proportion had dropped to one in fifty. Not only had the Orientals ceased to be a threat but once-fashionable racist ideas had been discredited by the practices of Nazi Germany.

Between 1947 and 1950 the structure of anti-Oriental laws which British Columbians had devised was dismantled. The barriers against Chinese immigration were lowered. The legal disabilities imposed on Chinese and Japanese were removed and, if otherwise qualified by age and citizenship, they received the franchise. In 1957, a Canadian of Chinese descent was elected to parliament.[41] These events took place with relatively little protest. Not even Mrs Glynn-Ward, who was then living in Victoria, raised her pen. The rabidly racist ideas about the Oriental 'menace' which had once been so common in British Columbia were anachronistic. *The Writing on the Wall*, once a topical propagandist tract, was a document from a past age.

NOTES

1 *The Vancouver Sun,* 23 Oct. 1921, 31; 12 Aug. 1921, 6. I have
  developed the theme of British Columbia's endeavours to inform
  eastern Canadians about the Oriental problem in 'Educating the
  "East"; British Columbia and the Oriental Question in the Interwar
  Years' *BC Studies* 18 (Summer 1973) 50-69.
2 For example, see Marilyn Barber, introduction to *Strangers Within
  Our Gates* by J.S. Woodsworth (Toronto 1972).
3 See my article, 'The Oriental "Menace" in British Columbia,' in S.M.
  Trofimenkoff, ed., *The Twenties in Western Canada* (Ottawa 1972)
  243-58.
4 See, for example, the testimony before Canada, Royal Commission
  on Chinese Immigration, *Report and Evidence* (Ottawa 1885) passim
  and Cheng Tien-Fang, *Oriental Immigration in Canada* (Shanghai
  1931) 37-8.
5 For a fuller treatment of the legal discriminations against Orientals
  see H.F. Angus, 'The Legal Status in British Columbia of Residents
  of Oriental Race and Their Descendants' *Canadian Bar Review* IX
  (Jan. 1931) 1-12. It should be noted that some legislation such as
  that relating to the acquisition of Crown lands did not apply to the
  Japanese because of treaty arrangements between Great Britain and
  Japan.
6 One of the more imaginative proposals was a regulation that the
  railway not be permitted to employ anyone who wore his hair more
  than 5½ inches long. Since most Chinese in British Columbia followed the custom of wearing a queue (pigtail), this would have
  excluded them effectively. The proposal did not get past first reading in parliament. Canada, Parliament, House of Commons, *Debates*
  (1878) 1067. After the Chinese Revolution of 1911-12, most
  Chinese abandoned this hair style.
7 Details on the riot may be found in R.E. Wynne, 'Reaction to the
  Chinese in the Pacific Northwest and British Columbia, 1850 to
  1910,' Ph D dissertation (University of Washington 1964) ch. 9;
  Howard H. Sugimoto, 'Japanese Immigration, The Vancouver Riots
  and Canadian Diplomacy,' unpublished ms (University of Washington
  1966); and C.J. Woodsworth, *Canada and the Orient* (Toronto 1941)
  72ff.

In August 1907, American agitators organized the Vancouver branch of the Asiatic Exclusion League, which was based in San Francisco and had branches in several American Pacific coast cities. In Vancouver, the League gained its initial support from trade unionists, but quickly got enthusiastic endorsations from leading members of both the Conservative and Liberal parties. By late September the League had 2000 paid-up members of whom about fifteen per cent were merchants or professional men (Wynne, 'Reaction to Chinese' 408).

8 Constitutionally, Mrs Glynn-Ward is also imprecise but it is not certain if her errors are deliberate literary techniques or the result of unfamiliarity with the political system. For example, as a member of the provincial legislature, Morley would have been known as an MLA, not an MP, and he would not have had the power to appoint an individual to the customs service (p 73). As premier, he would not have had the authority to appoint the lieutenant-governor or to make a binding recommendation to the federal government (p 105).

9 *Danger: The Anti-Asiatic Weekly* (20 Oct. 1921) 12

10 The most recent student of the episode has concluded that Dunsmuir's motives are still not clear. Mary E. Hallett, 'A Governor-General's Views on Oriental Immigration to British Columbia, 1904-1911' *BC Studies* 14 (Summer 1972) 57 n22.

11 The above paragraphs are based on Paul Phillips, *No Power Greater* (Vancouver 1967) passim.

12 *BC Federationist* (6 Jan. 1922) 2

13 In 1921 there were 544,464 acres of improved land in British Columbia. Economic Council of British Columbia, Research Department, *Statistics of Industry in British Columbia, 1871-1934* (Victoria 1935) Table A3

14 *Agricultural Journal* (July 1921) 114

15 For example, see the Royal Commission on Chinese Immigration, *Report* (1902) 18, 20, 68-9.

16 British Columbia, Legislative Assembly, *Votes and Proceedings* (31 Mar. 1920) 7-8; *Vancouver Daily Province* (27 May 1914) 5

17 For example, *Penticton Herald* (31 July 1919) 1; *Comox Argus* (14 Oct. 1920) 1

18 *Penticton Herald* (12 Oct. 1921) 3; *Cumberland Islander* (5 Nov. 1921) 4; *Nanaimo Free Press* (8 Nov. 1921) 2

19 See William Lyon Mackenzie King, *Report* ... [*on*] *Methods by Which Oriental Labourers* ... *Have Been Induced to Come to Canada* (Ottawa 1908).

20 J.A. Calder in Canada, Parliament, House of Commons, *Debates* (23 May 1921) 3828

21 Public Archives of Canada, Records of the Department of Immigration, RG76, Acc 70/47 File 815661, Percy Reid, memo for W.W. Cory (28 Apr. 1921)

22 J.A. Calder in Canada, Parliament, House of Commons, *Debates* (11 May 1921) 3207

23 Canada, Board of Review [Immigration], *Report* (1938) 13

24 *Vancouver World* (24 July 1913) 1, 4; (29 July 1913) 1

25 *Port Alberni News* (15 Oct. 1919) 2

26 Canada, Parliament, House of Commons, *Debates* (26 Apr. 1921) 2597. Italics mine

27 Lothrop Stoddard, *The Rising Tide of Color Against White World Supremacy* (New York 1923) 257, 301 [copyright 1920]. For the background of this book see John Higham, *Strangers in the Land* (New York 1967), 271-2. [copyright, 1955]. Stoddard had been strongly influenced by Madison Grant, whose *The Passing of the Great Race* had been published in 1916. I have not found any mention of Grant's work in the British Columbia press.

28 *Vancouver Daily Province* (2 Dec. 1919); 13; *Vancouver Sun* (11 Mar. 1914) 6

29 See A. Hiebert, 'The Oriental as He Appears in Some of the Novels of British Columbia' *BC Library Quarterly* 34 (Apr. 1971) 20-31

30 *Vancouver World* (7 Sept. 1921) 1

31 C.H. Young and Helen R.Y. Reid, *The Japanese Canadians* (Toronto 1939) 18-20

32 (15 Sept. 1921) 8

33 Canada, Parliament, House of Commons, *Debates* (16 Mar. 1949) 171

34 Foon Sien, 'Neither Three nor Four' *The New Citizen* (1 Mar. 1949) 2

35 *Vancouver Sun* (15 Apr. 1921) 2. After the novel was published, she spoke on the same subject to a joint meeting of the Board of Trade and Retail Merchants Association of Duncan. (*Cowichan Leader* [6 Oct. 1921] 1)

36 H. Glynn-Ward, *The Glamour of British Columbia* (New York & London: Century 1926) viii. This book was also published in Toronto by Macmillan in 1926 and by Doubleday, Doran in 1932.

37 In *Along the Road to Hazelton* (London nd) 48

38 *Victoria Colonist* (8 Oct. 1935) 4

39 *Victoria Times* (27 Dec. 1941) 16

40 *Victoria Colonist* (3 Feb. 1946) 17

41 As yet (1973), no Chinese or Japanese has been elected to the legislature of British Columbia though Canadians of Chinese and Japanese descent have held municipal office.

The writing on the wall

HILDA GLYNN-WARD

Original cover of *The Writing on the Wall* (Provincial Archives, Victoria, BC)

Part 1

The past

The story opens in the year 1910, and the opening scene is set in the suburbs of the city of Vancouver, in British Columbia.

Chapter 1

Introducing one Chung Lee and another man of parts

THE DAY WAS HOT and the road was dusty, so dusty that the gently trotting footsteps of Chung Lee made no sound at all, only left a little cloud behind to mark his progress.

It was the hour of siesta and there was no one in sight, only the blue-clad figure of Chung Lee jog-trotting soundlessly along the side of the Point Grey Road, a battered old straw hat on his head, the end of his pig-tail tucked away in his pocket, the heavy vegetable-baskets swaying back and front of him from the yoke on his shoulder.

He made no sort of effort to sell his wares, never turned aside to call at any of the houses, but kept straight on at the same unvarying pace, with his eyes on the ground, never even looking to the right or left of him. It almost seemed as though he were making for some definite destination.

A fat woman sitting on her verandah rocking to and fro and fanning herself called out to him as he passed.

'Got any fresh lettuces there, John? '

The Chinaman stopped and set his baskets down in front of her at the foot of the verandah steps.

'Pum-plums, cabbachee, wun-yuns by bunchee, applee, callatee, saladee by bunchee,' he chanted in a monotonous sing-song.

The bargain was made, Chung took up his baskets again and trotted on his way down the road. He did not stop again until he came to a house standing in a large garden enclosed in a board fence. He opened a door in the fence, went in, shut it carefully behind him and trotted up the garden path round to the back verandah.

He went up the steps to the kitchen door, which stood ajar, and here at last he set his baskets down.

Gordon Morley sat in his study with a cigar in his mouth, doing little sums on bits of paper and entering the resulting figures in account books. They must have been pleasant little sums, for there was no worried frown on his forehead such as men usually wear when they do their private accounts.

He was a big man in the prime of life, muscular, heavily built, with a driving force about him that showed itself in every movement. The build of his body was carried out again in his face, a fighting jowl with a long upper lip, heavy nose, eyes that missed nothing within range and precious little outside it.

But to the close observer there was a weakness somewhere, something lacking in all this super-abundance of personality, and it was difficult to say just why the close observer should get this impression when there was nothing but strength in every line of the face. Perhaps it was just this super-abundance of it all that did it, for to be really great a man must have a softness, and there was none in this face.

The mouth was hard to the point of selfishness – that was it, too much self. Gordon Morley knew no other gods but himself, he was therefore limited.

On this hot afternoon he was all alone in his house on the Point Grey Road. His wife was at some important women's luncheon in town and his son was at school. The woman who came to do the morning chores had long since gone.

So the master of the house sat at ease in his shirt-sleeves and did his pleasant little sums in peace. Through the open windows came the buzz of bees and the scent of many flowers from the garden.

Presently the sound of someone padding up the back verandah steps made the man writing put down his pen and lift his head to listen.

Came the monotonous chanting refrain in Chung Lee's metallic voice: 'Pum-plums, cabbachee, wun-yuns by bunchee, applee, callatee, saladee by bunchee – '

Gordon Morley went through to the kitchen and pushed the fly-door open. The Chinaman passed into the house, leaving his baskets outside. They went into the study and shut the door.

Mrs Gordon Morley sat drinking tea and discussing matters of moment with an acquaintance, Lizzie Laidlaw, in the 'Tea Kettle Inn.' The matron, fresh from the social triumphs of a smart club luncheon, was in a complacent and equable frame of mind. She arranged the folds of her rustling and obviously new dress with fingers fat and stubby but glistening with diamonds. The very weight of her large and ultra-fashionable hat seemed to call for a supercilious dignity of poise; she looked at her companion and every now and then at the tea-drinkers at other tables as though thanking her God she was not as they.

The woman with her was 'up from the country,' there was no mistake about that. The wholesome roses in her cheeks, the simplicity of her well-starched cotton dress and big, shady hat all bespoke the farm.

'Say, Liz,' remarked Mrs Morley, 'lots of the best people are selling out in the West End and starting in to build up on Shaughnessy Heights. Why ever don't you get your dad to sell out and buy a lot up there? You're just buried alive 'way down there in Lulu Island, never see anything, never go anywhere – '

'Dad sell out the farm?' cried Miss Laidlaw, horrified. 'Why, Dad wouldn't be Dad to think of such a thing, and me – I'd rather stay right where I am there on the farm than own all your old palaces on Shaughnessy Heights!'

Rose Morley looked at her friend as a successful commercial traveller might look at a cow munching hay.

'Well, each one to his taste, of course, but you don't realize one bit all you're missing. Look at *me*, now, before I married Gordon, working like a nigger down there on the farm – didn't know what life was beyond a basket social and a dance now and then, the sort we used to think fine in those days,' she gave a scornful laugh at the very memory.

'But now,' she went on, 'well, just see how we've got on since! I used to think it fine to own a house up at Fort Edward, even if it was small, but it was finer still to live in a first-class suite in town, and now we've got one of the dandiest houses on the Point Grey Road and pretty near every time you look in the papers you'll see Mrs Gordon Morley's name in the social news.'

'Well, Rose, I'm glad you're happy, and I'm glad I am too, but I think I'd rather see our best cow's name in the prize column of the exhibition news than my own in the social page! But now tell me some more about the luncheon. Who else was there?'

'Why, it was just the swellest function of the month; everybody was saying so. Mrs Bruce made the first speech. She told me after how her husband had made over $40,000 in four months in real estate deals, in South Vancouver, mostly. Just think of that! Say,

Liz, if you take my advice you'll buy a lot on the North Shore just opposite Hastings Park right now this afternoon, before you go home.'

'Oh, I don't think I'm specially interested in real estate, and Dad wouldn't like me to.' Lizzie Laidlaw placidly set her white teeth into another bit of cake.

'Well, you're losing the chance of a lifetime, that's all I can say. It's a dead sure thing. Gordon and I've both bought lots there and he says it's a cinch we'll make several thousands as soon as the Second Narrows bridge goes through.'

'But how do you know it is going through, Rose? They've been talking of it for years and it isn't through yet.'

'Well, it's a sure thing this time, anyway,' said Mrs Morley, decisively, 'and when everyone else is making fortunes Lizzie Laidlaw will have herself to thank if she gets left.'

'If so many people are *making* fortunes, Rose,' replied Lizzie, gently, '*someone* must be losing them. I'd just hate to make a pile of money out of someone else's loss.'

It was during the days of the real estate boom and fortunes were made and lost in less time than it took to add up the figures. A chance word in a tram-car of a vague rumor of some projected scheme was enough to flood the real estate offices with purchasers of lots in the vicinity in question. Men and women realized the sum total of their worldly goods and then staked their all on a 30 x 60-foot lot, seen only on a blue paper print in an agent's window.

Men who were broke to the world one week were seen the next driving round the park in a phaeton with a pair of trotters, and men who were in the habit of sailing their own steam yachts turned up in the offices of their friends to beg for a job.

Small wonder, then, that Mrs Morley shrugged her shoulders and turned the conversation.

'Even old Mrs McRobbie was there, and t'isn't often *she* turns out to anything now; she's getting on, you know. They say Carter's building the dandiest house over in Victoria for his mother, so I don't suppose I'll ever get into her set now she's going over there to live. Remember when Carter used to go to school with us down at Steveston, Liz? Then Old Man McRobbie made all that pile and the son was sent to school and college in the Old Country. My! but he was a lucky boy to come into all that money, wasn't he?'

'Well, Carter's not forgotten his old friends, anyway. He always comes in to have tea with us when he comes down our way duck-shooting.'

Rose Morley's jaw dropped with surprise. '*Does he?* You never told me that! '

'Well, no,' said Lizzie, busy with her gloves; 'it's not very interesting. Come, I want to buy some silk for a shirtwaist before I go home.'

They went out and walked up Granville Street together.

'Have you noticed,' enquired Lizzie, as they paused in front of one of the big Chinese shops, 'how big and flourishing these Chinese stores are now? I can remember, not so very long ago, when this one was a little two-by-four general store 'way down in Powell street. Then they moved up here and grew and grew till they're pretty near as big as Drysdale's, over the way.'

'Yes, but they sell the dandiest silks and cheaper than the all-white stores. Say, Liz, I'd like to have you come and visit with me a few days. When can you come? I'd take you about and it'd brighten you up a whole lot!'

The other woman looked up the street and then down the street before she replied, uncomfortably, 'It's real kind of you, Rose, and I'd like to come fine, but Dad would never let me. You see, he's never forgiven Gordon.'

'Never forgiven Gordon!' repeated Gordon's wife. 'For the love o' Mike, what for, Lizzie?'

'*For selling his farm to those Chinamen, Rose!*'

Chapter 2

In which Gordon Morley tells no secrets

NEXT TO HIMSELF the only thing in the world that Gordon Morley cared about was his son, the reason perhaps being that to all outward appearances the boy was cast in the same identical mould as his father.

When Mrs Morley returned home she found the two sitting together looking at a picture book on the verandah, the boy on his father's knee. She sat heavily down beside them, overcome with the heat.

'Bobbie, have you done your home lessons?' she asked, a little sharply.

'Oh, Mother, just let me stay a bit longer out here, it's so nice and cool!'

'Sure, leave the boy stay a bit Rose,' said his father. 'You tell us about your club luncheon.'

'You're as soft as soft with the boy, Gordon; he'll never get on if he doesn't work harder,' grumbled the woman, as she took her hat off and threw it on a chair beside her, but the grievance was soon forgotten as she warmed up to a detailed account of her afternoon.

Her husband listened with the careful interest he gave to everything, great and small, that came within his ken.

'So Bruce made all that much, eh? Does he still keep his wife pretty short?'

'Why, I don't know. What makes you think so? Anyway, she's got enough to plunge pretty heavy in the North Vancouver scheme. I told her of that and she was tickled to death.'

'You told her it was inside information, didn't you?'

'Sure, Gordon. I'd like to buy another lot or two myself before they all go.'

'I'd buy somewhere else if I were you. Don't ever put all your eggs in one basket.'

'But that's a cinch about the bridge, isn't it, Gordon?' cried Mrs Morley, in some anxiety. 'Why, you said so over and over again!'

'Sure, it's a cinch. Don't get so panicky – I only say it's a mistake to put all your eggs in one basket. Tell me what you did after the lunch?'

'I met Lizzie Laidlaw in town and we had tea together. She's dull! Why, she's well past thirty and getting quite homely – lost all her looks, if she ever had any. She won't ever get a husband now, not even if she had the chance to meet one, which she hasn't sticking down there in that hole-in-the-corner farm!'

'Oh, come! She's a cuddlesome kind of a piece so far as I can remember her.'

'Is that so?' said the wife, with irritation in her tone. 'Well, maybe so when you saw her ten or twelve years ago. Come on in, Bobbie, and get to your lessons at once!' She rose as she spoke and went in through the open window to the study. She was passing through the room to the door when something arrested her attention, and she paused with her head up, sniffing.

'What a nasty smell there is in here, Gordon!' she called out. 'Whatever is it? It smells just like an escape of acetylene gas!'

A shade of annoyance passed over the face of the man outside. He rose and went in to her.

'I smell nothing. Nothing at all. Why, it must be in your own nose! Come, I'm awful hungry; let's have some tea.' He opened the door, and linking his arm in hers, drew her towards the kitchen, laughing at her protestations about the smell.

'I have a bit of news for you, but I shan't tell you till tea's ready,' he said.

Very soon the little family was seated round the table, tea was poured out and the wife all agog to hear what her husband had to tell her.

'I'm going to stand for parliament at this next election.'

A bombshell bursting beside her could hardly have had more effect on Rose Morley. The color suffused her face – she sat silent, thinking, letting the news soak into ther brain until she felt almost dizzy with the pictures her imagination conjured up. She had not spent a dozen years with Gordon Morley without knowing that he succeeded in everything he touched, and her faith in his ability was as a dog's faith in his master.

Therefore she already saw herself as the wife of an MP, with all the prestige of position and power, queening it over her friends, and rising, ever rising to the very top of heights hitherto undreamed of. Yes, Rose Morley knew her husband. 'Oh, Gordon!' she gasped. 'Who is putting you up?' 'A whole bunch of them. Some you know – George Worrall, Craddock Low, Tom Squires – and some you don't.' 'George Worrall!' exclaimed his wife, in surprise. 'What pull has he got, away up there at Cedar Cottage?' 'Now, use your brains! Think! He's road superintendent, ain't he, for a pretty big district? Well, don't he control the daily bread-and-butter for a good few voters, eh?'

A gleam of appreciative understanding spread over Mrs Morley's face.

'And what's he going to get out of it?'

'Hadn't you better wait and see? You'd find it a sight easier than keeping your mouth shut now,' and Gordon Morley helped himself to salad.

His wife glanced at him and then leisurely poured herself out another cup of tea.

'I *have* heard tell of such things as wives helping their husbands in little byways in the political world. I don't see why you should take it for granted that I should be an exception to the rule.'

Morley looked quizzically over at his wife as he answered.

'Well, Rosy, it's not as if you were the tittle-tattler most women are, and if you'll promise me never to tell anybody outside this house anything without first asking me, why, I'll show you lots of ways you can help us both up to the top o' the tree.'

Gordon Morley had long since made it a rule to tell his wife only the things he wanted spread abroad or things she was bound to find out for herself – and to tell them in the form of dead secrets.

This pleased everybody and answered his purposes excellently.

'George Worrall, of all people!' mused his wife, as she sipped her tea. 'Well, what *does* he expect to get out of it, Gordon?'

'I'll tell you. One of the planks of our party is *"Good roads and more of them for the farmer-settlers."* It's a crying shame that all that rich country up round Agassiz, for instance, is unavailable for settlers because there are no roads through it. We are going to make it our business if we get in, to make more roads, beginning with one up there that's badly needed. There are good farmers who've bought up there and can't settle on their lots because there are no roads.'

This was all perfectly true. Yet Morley refrained from telling his wife that these particular farmers who were clamoring for roads in this particular district were Chinamen who had brought a mixture of bribery and pressure to bear on the subject.

'I see,' she said. 'So Worrall will get a bigger road job if you get in. How clever of you, Gordon!'

Again he refrained from telling her that the contract for this road was already let — on certain conditions — to George Worrall.

'But Craddock Low — how can he help you? He's only a lawyer.'

'Yes, but the cutest lawyer in Vancouver. Folk are frightened of him. They say he can see through a brick wall, and make a parson swear he saw something that didn't happen. He's got four or five big lawsuits on now between big companies, and each of them has to stand well with him. He knows more secrets of the past histories — yes, and present, too — of Vancouver folk than anyone else in BC. Oh, yes, he controls a good few votes!'

'Funny! What's *he* going to get out of it, I wonder? I didn't know you'd been seeing anything of him lately. I saw Mrs Low at the luncheon. She made me die laughing telling me how they had to go, him and her, to some grand dinner in their honor at a rich Chinaman's down near Main Street. She said it was so swagger and yet so funny! You know he defends most of the Chinese cases that come up in the courts, and they have to entertain all kinds.'

Yes, Gordon Morley knew. But he waived the question. He pushed his chair back and lit his pipe.

'It's a good idea,' he said, 'to have the cutest lawyer in BC back of us. Very well. Then there's Tom Squires — he's a pretty smart real estate man, as you know, and has made his pile out of it. He's been interested in North Vancouver property for some time, and as we are going to make the Second Narrows bridge one of the chief planks of our party — well, you know what effect that'll have on property over there, so it's up to him to back us for all he's worth.'

'Of course! But, Gordon, I must say I really can't understand why you've only bought *one* lot over there and won't let me buy any more, when we might have made a young fortune out of it.'

'Well, surely you can see that it doesn't look well for an MP to be making use of private information to fill his own pockets. Just one lot each and no one can say anything. We take our chance along with the others.'

Morley said this with the unction of a Sunday school teacher moralizing to a class of small boys. His wife had not the glimmer of a suspicion that when she had bought her lot on the North Shore she bought it from her own husband. She could not know that when the prospect of a bridge across the Second Narrows had first been mooted it had been adversely reported upon by a Dominion Government engineer who had been bribed to hold back his report by certain men until after the elections.

That the men who had bribed him were Gordon Morley, Tom Squires and another, and that these three men had immediately bought up all the land round the projected site for the bridge, and had employed another agent to sell it again in small lots at an enormous profit to a gullible public who were only too willing to believe that the next government would see the longed-for bridge put through.

She could not therefore know that the money she and others had paid for these lots might as well have been thrown into the sea for all the good to come of it during their lifetime. Morley had allowed his wife to buy and had bought himself in order to throw aside suspicion. As he had already made many thousands out of the scheme he could afford to throw away two or three hundreds.

'There's no need for you to worry about money, old girl,' he told her now. 'I've got more'n you'll want to buy a few new dresses with, so go along and buy 'em, and tell me how much you want. I'd like to see you show up at all the society functions you can get in from now on, see! It'll help.'

Rose came over and put her arm across her husband's shoulders.

'You surely are the cleverest, cutest old boy that ever was, aren't you? And now, Gordon, do let's have a China-boy to do the cooking instead of a white woman. They get through ten times more work, and besides, it's so much smarter! All the best people have one now.'

Morley patted her hand and turned to pick up a broken engine that his son was playing with on the floor.

'You know what I said, Rose — *no China-boy ever comes into my house!* I said so before and I'm the same man as I was then, so put that idea out of your head.'

Chapter 3

Which introduces Lizzie Laidlaw

LIZZIE LAIDLAW SAT at the kitchen door picking over red currants for jam. The sun was low in the west and it sent shafts of yellow light to make patterns on the kitchen floor and rest like a halo on the fair coils of the woman's hair.

The evening, quiet and cloudless, was filled with the peaceful sounds of home, the drowsy hum of bees in the hollyhocks, the tinkle of cow-bells far across the fields, and at times the well-loved voice of her father calling the cows home; the racket of milk-cans across the yard as the hired man prepared for milking, and a late mother-hen crooning her chicks to sleep.

Lizzie's hands were busy enough, but her eyes, placid as a mountain lake at sunset, looked out rather wistfully at the distant horizon. Presently, however, their expression changed from vagueness to attention. She saw something. Out of the distance, winding its way along a foot-track between fields of standing grain came the figure of a man on horseback.

Long before the rider became recognizable to anyone else, the healthy glow on the girl's face had deepened to a flush and the firm lines of her mouth had broken into a little smile of pleasure. Nearer and nearer he came till he was close enough to wave his hat to her; then he stopped to exchange a few words of greeting with her father. At last he rode into the yard, tied up his horse and came across to her.

It appeared that they knew each other too well for the usual formal greeting, for they met as though they had never parted.

'I thought you'd have been up north at the cannery by now,' she said, as he sat himself down on the step at her feet.

'I should be, but I couldn't go without seeing you again, Liz,' and he caught hold of one of her busy, currant-stained hands and kissed it.

'It'll be fine up north just now,' she said; 'so cool and nice sailing amongst the islands and up the inlets in that lovely launch of yours!'

The man leant forward and looked eagerly into her face. 'Yes, and it's all yours for the say-so, Liz, the launch and the life and myself. What pleasure is there in anything for me if I haven't got you to share it with! *Life is not worth living without you! I've waited for twelve years – how much longer must I wait?'* he cried, passionately.

The woman's face had grown drawn and white and her lips were tightly pressed together to subdue the tremble in them. She put out her hand and passed it soothingly over the man's head.

'Carter McRobbie,' she said, and her voice had tears in it, 'don't be tempting me again! My answer will be always the same so long as ever Dad's here. I'll no leave him for anyone, not even for you. But I'm no keeping you, my man. Why won't you go and pick some bonnie lassie that'll make you a better wife than I would?'

McRobbie brushed the suggestion impatiently aside and rested his head moodily on his hand.

'What's an old farm compared with a man's life!' he muttered.

'*This* farm *is* a man's life! Dad came here when he was but a lad and found a wilderness, and he has spent his life in turning it into a fertile farm – the sort of farm the country depends on for its very existence. The farm and me is just all he's got left now, and he can't stay here without me and it would kill him to leave it.'

'Does your father never wonder why you haven't married, Liz? He'd be the last man to keep you – if he knew.'

'And I'm trusting to your honor not to speak of it to him,' she answered, gently.

'None are so blind –'

'Hush, Carter, he's coming!' Lizzie rose and was gathering up her apron with all the currant stalks in it when her father came round the corner.

Robert Laidlaw was nearly seventy, but still so straight and tall that he could easily pass for ten years younger. He was of that fine old hardy type of pioneer that has laid the corner stones of the British Empire, loyal to the core, single-minded and cleanly of life and purpose, with an abiding scorn for those small souls whose greed of personal gain is their one ambition.

Many a man had felt his soul stripped bare before the searing directness of Robert Laidlaw's eyes, and shamed that the other should see his own paltriness, had slunk away to hide.

'Well, lass, how soon can ye get tea? I'm ready and Carter'll be hungry after his ride.'

'A few minutes, Dad! You sit down and talk while I get it.'

The old man drew a chair out onto the verandah and sat down beside McRobbie.

'And how's the salmon coming in up at Rivers Inlet this season, eh, boy? A good catch of sockeye this year?'

'Never better! The trouble is, we can't get hands enough to deal with it.'

'Why, aren't there enough West Coast Indians for you up there?'

'No — or rather, there would be if one could depend on them, but you can't. They promise one man and if the next comes along with a higher offer they forget their promise and work for him. If it wasn't for the klootchmen to fill the cans I'd get rid of all those lazy devils of Indians. But in future I'm going to increase the number of Chinese in the cannery and fill all my boats with Japs. The difficulty is that everybody wants them, but I think I've struck an idea that'll solve the problem now.'

'I'm sorry to hear you say so, my boy. I'd rather see you employ whites or Indians. Everyone that employs Chinamen is the means, direct or indirect, of bringing more of them into the country, and God knows that we are overrun with them enough already.'

'Oh, well,' replied Carter, carelessly, 'they make cheap labor, and that's what we want in BC, don't we?'

'*Cheap labor! Cheap labor!*' exclaimed the old man, sitting forward and thumping his fist on the arm of his chair. 'Their "cheap labor" is going to cost you dear and *cost your children their country, young man*, if you let it go on. The gates have been opened wide and they are pouring in at such a rate that the country will be flooded if the white men can't be brought to open their eyes to the danger.'

'But they've done their best to stop it by putting a head-tax on them, and a law was made two years ago to make it difficult for a Chinaman to buy land, so they can't really get much hold here.'

'*Head-tax nothing!* That has *helped* to bring them in; it made an extra incentive for Chinese capitalists to form companies which brought their men in by the hundred, paid their head-taxes in lump sums down to the government, and then got it back plus fifty per cent interest from the wages the men earned during the next few years. Why, the head-tax has made more Chinese millionaires than there'll ever be white ones in BC! As for that land law you speak of, made by a handful of dog-gone hypocrites of MP's to save their face – a Chinaman may not buy land *direct* from the Government, but indirectly the law allows him to buy it from anyone else.'

The old man shook his head so vigorously that his long, white beard quivered to the very tips.

'I doubt if they are buying very much, just a small holding here and there,' said the other.

'Carter McRobbie, *open your eyes, man!* Look round and see how many yellow men are renting land that was farmed by whites a year or so ago. And renting is next step to buying, in most cases. Look where that son-of-a-gun Gordon Morley sold out his forty-acre bit near here to them! The traitorous calf-worshipper, selling his birthright to a yellow man!'

'Did you know he's to stand for parliament at the next elections?'

'That so? Then God pity the country, for he'd sell it to the devil for a thousand dollars cash! And *he'll get in*, by hook or crook he'll get in! I know the refuse he's made of. ... Then again, look at Victoria, with an even bigger Chinatown than we have here, and in the best part of the city, too. Rich Chinamen's houses in the best residential parts! You know that as well as I do. ... I hear they're beginning to rent big stretches of land up Agassiz way, seven or eight of them together in a combine, and they'll beat the white man to it at his own game, you mark my words!'

The scent of mignonette filled the air and the homely chink of milk pails, the voice of the hired man as he spoke now and then to the cows, the quick, light step of Lizzie as she moved to and fro in the house – all these things were stamped indelibly on Carter's mind as in after years the memory of this evening came back to him. Moodily he sat staring into space while Robert Laidlaw went on talking.

'You have the gift of money, my boy, and money is power. See to it that ye don't misuse that same! It's up to such as you to save your country for your own nation, let alone your own race, remember that! But you're all *drifting* now, yea, *drifting*, slowly but surely. Look at the numbers of Chinese vegetable gardens – fifteen years more and the *white man won't be allowed to grow a vegetable.* Look at the increasing number of Chinese laundries – now, they work for you, but a few years hence and *your children will be working for their children.* They're creeping into everything – trade and labor, gardening and farming, lumber even, and in every case *they're beating us at our own game!'*

'Well, you've got to blame the CPR, Mr Laidlaw. They brought 'em in in the first place and they've got to get 'em out or keep 'em under.'

'There's no keeping 'em under now – *it's too late.* They'll go forward from now on as slowly and surely as the tide comes in until –'

The younger man broke in with an unexpected remark.

'I shouldn't have thought the Chinese were such a menace to us as the Japs are. They are away cleverer and have more need of new colonies.'

'You're right, Carter, boy, you're right. I don't like to see these Japs fishing our waters as they are doing. It's their own national trade and the climate's just the same, so everything's in their favor, even our own fishing laws. You cannery men must keep your weather eye open for the Japs, Carter.'

Lizzie's voice calling them both in to tea interrupted the discourse and they went in to the big, cool kitchen. Home-baked scones and a home-cured ham, lusciously pink, the sheen of blue willow-pattern plates, red fruit and thick yellow cream, the rays of the setting sun making patterns on the tablecloth through the cucumber-vine leaves on the verandah, and the low, sweet voice of the woman he loved making homely conversation to glaze over the ache in two hearts.

A bitter-sweet kiss hastily snatched and a man rode away from that house across the fields of standing grain with unseeing eyes and a heart filled with bitterness against the man who was the unconscious obstacle to the one thing that made life worth the living, the one thing that his money could not buy.

Chapter 4

In which the 'Empress' unships a valuable cargo

A DARK NIGHT and no moon, a warm, wet, gusty wind and a storm blowing up from the Pacific. The storm cone was already hoisted at Prospect Point to warn outgoing boats, and there were white-horses at play all over the gulf.

The *Empress of Japan* ploughed her way over the sea towards the mainland with a bone in her mouth.

But Chung Lee was pleased at the look of the weather; it suited him and his purposes admirably. He had trotted across from Pender Street to the waterfront more than once that evening to look at the sky and over at the North Shore, and had nodded complacently to himself as he trotted back again.

Back to his lair to get his vegetable baskets, into which he flung some cabbages and lettuces rather the worse for wear, and set the yoke on his shoulders. Down Pender Street he trotted, turning south up a by-street where the sight of a belated Chink with a few vegetables he had failed to sell excited no attention at all. On he padded softly, tirelessly, swiftly, until he reached the Granville bridge, over this turning sharp to the right he skirted the shores of the Indian Reserve. On and on until at last he came to a waste of land, tall tufted grass and thickets of scrub willow and poplar, quiet and deserted as a race-course on a mid-December night.

Here there stood — and stands still — an ancient wharf, long since forgotten and out of use for any purpose whatsoever; and here on the shore in the shadow of it Chung Lee set down his baskets and sat him down to wait patiently, stoically, as those of the East wait, with never a shadow of an expression on his thick and stolid face and never an extra gleam of expectancy in his narrow little pig eyes.

As for an hour or more he waited, the wind died down a bit and the bluster and splash of the waves grew less and less. It began to rain a little. Out of the silence round came the faint chug-chug of a gasoline launch. Nearer and nearer it came, louder and louder, until at last the outline of it rounding the point became discernible to the watcher.

On came the little boat towards the wharf. The man aboard shut down her engines and steered her alongside. He moored, and now the waiting Chinaman rose and hurried like a shadow along the wharf to the boat.

The man aboard evidently expected him, for he held up a lantern so that Chung Lee might find his foothold as he let himself down into the launch, and the lantern lit up the heavy features of Gordon Morley, potential MP.

Scarcely a word passed between the two as the engine was started up and the launch chug-chugged its way out to sea again.

By the time the *Empress of Japan* had reached Point Atkinson and was heading for the Narrows, there were three people aboard who were watching and waiting for her to slow down, as ships do before passing through the gateway into port. One was the captain, the other was the third officer on the bridge, whose special duty it was to watch, and the other was Sin Lung, one of the Chinese cooks in the galley, who was stealthily and tremendously busy over certain concerns of his. These concerns looked like white canvas sacks containing each a 60-pound weight of little copper cans and a multitude of corks. He was busy tying a long rope onto the neck of each sack and he seemed scared to death lest anyone should see him.

Every now and then since leaving Point Atkinson he had looked out of a port hole anxiously, and once when he looked he saw the thing he wished to see, for he became busier than ever with his sacks and looked no more. All that the third office on the bridge saw was a small gasoline launch chugging along in the rain parallel with the *Empress* and rather close in, with a light that was evidently a lantern carried by a man who was walking about on deck. He rather thought what dam-fools they were to come so close, on account of the wash – some belated fishermen, no doubt; then he forgot all about them in the interest of passing through the Narrows.

Sin Lung made sure once again that no one was looking, then he hurried his bundles along to the garbage chute, thrust them down it one by one, keeping the rope attached to each in his hand until he felt it had reached the sea – to preclude any chance of a splash that might reach the ears of the far too watchful third officer. This done and when the last sack had disappeared Sin Lung stood back and wiped the beads of perspiration off his brow with the sleeve of his coat.

The *Empress of Japan* steamed on her way, leaving $20,000 worth of opium bobbing about in her wake.

Ten minutes afterwards it was picked up and counted by Gordon Morley and Chung Lee. A quarter of an hour later Chung Lee was trotting gently back to Chinatown with it concealed under the vegetables in his baskets, and the gasoline launch was back at her moorings off Point Grey. All quite simple. In fact, *'the skids were greased.'*

The Chief of Police and Robert Hart, detective, both in plain clothes, were hastening along the Magee Road out to Kerrisdale in a car.

When eventually they stopped and Hart got out with his ears full of the detailed instructions of the Chief anent watching a certain house with his eyes peeled until he was relieved, the Chief turned his car round and again came to a stop beside Hart, who had stood still to watch him.

'By the way, Hart, I'm real sorry you won't be with us tonight, we're going to have a great old time; but this job'll keep you fixed right here. We're going to make a midnight raid down in Chinatown on that yellow devil, Chung Lee.'

The effect on Hart of this bit of information was curious, but the Chief was busy with his clutch, and anyway, had he seen he might have interpreted the other's expression as annoyance at being left out of the fun.

'Why, have you had any special news?'

'Well, the *Japan* came in last night and if she brought any stuff it's right here now. They're getting it into the country somehow, but Lord only knows how — it fair beats me!'

'Have you found out anything about Chung Lee?'

'Nothing definite, only we know he's the wiliest fish that ever slipped off our hooks. The trouble is they stand by each other too well. If you look for one Chung Lee you find a dozen of the same name, and they're all so blamed alike. Funny, Rawlins met a Chink on his beat last night, about three in the morning, with vegetables. It struck him it was a queer time for him to be around so he stopped him. Said he could have sworn it was Chung Lee, but when he said the name

the man looked blank and said, "Me Sin Loo, no savvy Chung Lee!"
So what can you do?"

With that the Chief drove off. Hart was in a hole, a pretty desperate hole. A block away was the house he was to watch, and in
five minutes he was to be there 'on duty' until further notice. Once
there he would have no chance and no time to get himself out of the
hole, and this meant ruin.

It meant the bitter enmity and rancour of two very powerful
men, men to whom he was beholden for his position, men who knew
too much about him and his past history and his real name. It meant
the loss of acceptable little presents, of his present job certainly, and
it meant the incurring of a vengeance that would follow him wher-
ever he went.

And these two men were in blissful ignorance of the news he had
just heard, news that was of terribly vital importance to them. He
looked around him, frowning; the long summer evening was already
drawing to a close. It was 9 o'clock and there was little light left. No
such thing as a public telephone about.

He took the only course and started at a run down the road to a
point where he knew there was a little all-sorts store. Fortunately it
was still open, so he calmed himself to walk in casually.

'Bag o' Bull Durham, please, ma'am,' he said to the woman who
came out of the room behind.

'Sorry, we're just out of it. Anything else you'd like instead?'

'Oh, well, I'll take a packet o' Player's instead!' He fumed at the
delay while she got change and talked politely of the weather. He
made as if to go, but turned with his hand on the door latch.

'Say, would you let me use your 'phone?'

'Why, sure, if you don't mind coming through. We're havin' our
supper, but you needn't mind!'

He followed her into the room. It seemed he had never seen so
large a family in all his life. Cursing them for existing, with a polite
smile on his face he crossed to the 'phone and gave a number in as
low a voice as he could.

It was a woman who answered him.

'Say, is your husband at home?' he asked.

'Why, yes, but he's just outside starting up the car. We're going
out. Can I give any message?'

'I must speak to him before he goes. Say it's important.'

An interval elapsed. Then a man's voice on the 'phone — the voice of Gordon Morley.

'Are you coming out tonight?' asked Hart.

'Who's speaking?'

'Well, don't you recognize the voice of your best friend?' said Hart, slowly and distinctly, and trying to sound facetious for the benefit of the listening family.

'No, I don't. Why don't you say your name? I'm in a hurry.'

'You heard it in Winnipeg and before that in Seattle, *and the hurry you are in now is nothing to the hurry you're going to be in!* Are you coming out tonight?'

At last Morley seemed to sense something wrong. His next question was to the point.

'Where to and when?'

'Oh, well, we'll say the corner of Mactavish and Twenty-third, if that suits you. I'll be waiting, and a quarter of an hour from now if you can make it!'

An exclamation came over the 'phone, and then another question: 'Are you sure it's important?'

'As dead sure as eggs is eggs and *sacks is sacks!*' said Hart, with a laugh.

This appeared to be definite enough for the other, who shut off the 'phone in a hurry, and Hart got up and bowing his thanks he let himself out of the room, out of the house, and once clear started off into the darkness with the speed of a hare with a greyhound after it.

A quarter of an hour late, but the Chief would never know that.

Chapter 5

In which a famous lawyer finds himself in a hurry

ROSE MORLEY WAS impatient at the delay. It seemed to her a silly, pointless conversation that her husband was holding on the 'phone. But when he put down the receiver he looked so cross and preoccupied that she refrained from saying anything; she particularly wanted to keep his temper unruffled so that she might enjoy this dance to the full. She had been looking forward to the Craddock Low's dance.

Morley said nothing. He hurried his wife into the car and went round to crank the engine. There was some difficulty in starting it and he swore roundly. But they were off at last and driving at a far more unwary speed than he usually drove, down the Point Grey road and over the Granville bridge towards the West End.

As they neared the Craddock Low's house on Beach Avenue, Morley turned to his wife and said to her, 'Sorry, Rose, I can't come in with you now. I've got to go and meet a man and I'm late already. I'll join you later. Make some excuse for me.'

Mrs Morley was thoroughly annoyed, and she said so this time in very plain terms.

But her husband interrupted her roughly.

'Don't be a fool, Rose! It's to do with the elections. This chap's asked me for help and if I refuse him it's like as not I lose a good many votes.'

This put a rather different complexion on the matter, and he was allowed to go without further ado. He sped away towards Kerrisdale as far as he dared drive, but even so it was a quarter to ten when he reached the appointed place.

As he drew up his car at the corner of the two streets Hart stepped out from the shadows and came to his side.

'You'll have to get a move on, Gordon. They're going to raid Chung Lee's place at midnight. It's up to you to get a warning to him before that. I'm stuck here watching that house. The Chief brought me down himself and he only let it slip about the raid just as he was leaving!'

Morley let out some whispered and vitriolic curses.

'What do they suspect? How much do they know?' he asked.

'Only the same old suspicion of Chung and the fact of the *Empress* coming in last night. I don't think they suspect anyone else – yet!'

'But couldn't you have got away from here to Chinatown yourself without the Chief knowing?'

'Not on your life! I might have been seen down there, and besides, he's sending a man to relieve me here and he didn't say the time. You don't know the Chief!'

Yes, Morley knew him quite well; he was either crassly obtuse or irritatingly incorruptible.

'Well, damn it, I guess I got to go myself!'

'There's nothing else for it, an' what's more, you got to look slippy! It's near ten now!'

Morley slipped in the clutch and moved off. He drove faster than ever he had driven before, tempted by the lack of traffic at this hour, the fact that the car was running smoothly and the desperate hurry he was in. All went well until he was over the Granville bridge, when suddenly deciding to turn right and go down one of the side streets instead, he swerved unexpectedly and a boy coming behind him on a bicycle was knocked flat and under the wheels before he knew it.

Mad with irritation, Morley turned off the switch and jumped out to see what had happened. He drew the boy out from underneath and found him unconscious. As ill-luck would have it, a policeman had seen the incident and came running up, with the result that Morley and his car were ordered to drive the policeman and the boy to the nearest police station.

A doctor was summoned and Morley detained. There was no way out of it, he had to stay. Moreover he had, as a potential MP, to pretend the greatest concern for the boy's condition, which interested him not a bit, the while his mind worked at feverish haste to find a way out of the difficulty.

Half-past ten, and only an hour and a half in which to warn Chung and give him time to get into hiding and leave no trace of all damning evidence behind, evidence enough to lead to the betrayal of not only himself, Morley, but others, Craddock Low especially. Ah, an idea! He would 'phone Low to come down at once and make him go bail for him.

The police offered no objection to his 'phoning a friend, but as to bail — well, the doctor had just come. They would see what he said. There was delay in bringing Mr Craddock Low to the 'phone. He was dancing and surrounded by guests. When he did come he proved stupendously dense as to the need for hurry, and Morley, in the same predicament at the other end as Hart had been an hour earlier, found it difficult to make himself convincing with an audience of unsympathetic police listening to every word.

It was getting on for 11 PM when Low turned up. He commiserated with his friend in a shocked tone and expressed much anxiety as to the boy's condition, but as the police politely but firmly refused to allow bail, at any rate until after the doctor's report, he didn't see how he could be of any use.

Morley managed to draw him aside and whispered a few words into his ear which brought beads of perspiration out on his forehead. The doctor came out, reporting that the boy's condition was precarious; he was still unconscious and the ambulance was to be kept waiting a little longer.

'They won't let me go yet,' whispered Morley, drawing Low aside again. '*You'll have to go,* and *lose no time!* They said midnight and that may mean any time after 11. Take my car!'

'But, damn it, man, *I* can't drive a car! I'll have to beat it now, running all the way. What a devil of a fix!'

There was nothing for it, as he said, but to run, though first of all he had to get himself out of the police station quietly and without special hurry, as became the best-known barrister in British Columbia. He had to walk with dignity until he had put several blocks between himself and the police station, and then, not till then, was he able to show signs of hurry. He buttoned his light overcoat lightly across to hide his evening suit, turned up his trousers, rumpled his hair over his forehead and pulled down his cap as far as it would go.

Then he set off at a quick trot in the direction of Chinatown. He was out of condition and altogether unused to violent exercise, but there was much at stake. Once a policeman called after him, but he didn't look round, and again he heard footsteps following and made a detour round a block to escape them. Once down in Pender Street he felt easier. Here the sight of a man running brought no surprise to the wooden yellow faces that glided past him. Everywhere little black-clad men shuffled along soft-footed and swift, leaving as they passed a foul whiff of stale opium on the heavy, evil air that was almost tangible with smells of the East.

There were few lights and the murky shadows seemed alive. Here and there were signs illuminated above chop-suey houses, a theatre, flaring restaurants, little shops still open showing a medley of barrels and ginger-jars, open boxes of cheap Western goods side by side with Eastern comfits in lurid pink paper, strings of dried fish and faded vegetables. Low became conspicuous because of his European dress, which was a rarity in those days in the heart of Chinatown.

As he passed the shuttered windows, with gleaming chinks of light between the cracks, he could heard the chanting gabble of many Chinamen busy at fantan or chuk-a-luk. Presently he stopped and with a hasty look up and down the street, turned up an alley-way which was no more than a dark slit between two tumble-down houses. It was so dark he had to feel his way along the wall; his coat brushed the walls on either side as he walked.

Far up on the left his groping hands came in contact with a door handle, which he turned stealthily, but it was, as he expected, locked. He tapped on the door in a certain way with the tips of his nails and waited, panting. Soft living and much rich food had deadened his capacity for physical emergency, so his wind was gone and his face was mottled and blue.

Someone within opened the door slowly to the width of one inch, so slowly that the uninitiated might not have noticed it open-ing, particularly as the aperture revealed no light, the darkness within being blacker than the darkness without. But Low knew from experience that there was someone there waiting for him to give a sign. He rubbed his finger-nails against his teeth. The door was opened wide enough for him to pass in, and shut and barred again instantly behind him.

For all other sound he might have been alone in the thick, velvety darkness, and although he had been so many a time before, the delay this time set his nerves on edge.

'*Take me to Chung, quick!*'

A moment in the darkness, a match was struck and held up to his face, while a pair of narrow, slanting eyes examined him. Apparently satisfied, the other turned with a muttered 'Allitee, you follow,' and opened a door back of him. He picked up a dingy hurricane-lamp that had been turned low and was both smoking and smelling badly.

They passed through several rooms full of what looked like junk, chiefly barrels, through one lighted up, showing half a dozen Chinamen sitting round a table throwing dice. They looked up as Low and his leader passed through, showing little concern or surprise, along a passage in the middle of which the Chinaman set down his lantern and pulled up some boards in the floor, disclosing a flight of steps downwards. Low went first, his leader carefully replacing the boards after him.

Down, down into the underground they went till the wooden steps gave place to ones beaten out of the very earth. Of three passages they took the middle one. There were smoky oil lamps hanging from the roof that just succeeded in changing blackness into gloom.

Twisting round for some unaccountable reason, the tunnel stopped short at a door, whereon the leader knocked with his nails, the same knock given by Low at the outer door. It was opened just as carefully, but revealed a light within and at the same time let out an atmosphere so nauseatingly foul that the unaccustomed would have turned back sick and faint. Low, however, passed in and the door shut behind him.

It was a long room with lamps hanging from the ceiling, and the walls were lined with rows of bunks, each of which contained a corpse-like figure, stark naked, and all in different stages of the influence of the God of Narcotics. Some pulled at their long pipes, others just lay back and stared with dull, unseeing eyes at the ceiling; others again seemed quite dead. None took the least interest in the newcomer; they were beyond things of outside interest. The floor of the den was littered with filth indescribable, and the stench of cesspools rose to meet the soul-killing fumes of opium.

On a long, low table in the middle stood little contrivances with burning flames beneath them, and at the end of the table sat the man who had carried his vegetables to the door of Morley's house in the Point Grey Road, the man that had waited so patiently for the launch at the deserted wharf – Chung Lee.

Craddock Low's few hasty words directly he was inside the room had the effect of a magician's wand in changing the somnolent aspect of things. Chung was outside the door in a second whistling loud and long through his fingers, and immediately the passage was alive with Chinamen running from all quarters, springing, it seemed, out of the earth itself.

Each to his appointed place like well-rehearsed fire-drillers on a big liner – no confusion, no scurry, little noise. The prostrate opium eaters were carried off down another passage at the other end of the room, every trace of opium and pipes vanished, the mattresses on the bunks were replaced by boxes of merchandise so that the bunks looked like shelves in a storeroom.

'*The papers, Chung!*' exclaimed Low. '*Have you got them? For God's sake don't leave them behind!*'

'Them safe now, you no savvy Chung!'

'A light, then! Let me out the way I came. Quick! They may be here any time now!'

They went up the stairs again, but it was too late. Far overhead they heard shouts, scuffling trampling and the tap-tap of a stick that sounded for concealed doors and cubby-holes.

Low looked round Wildly. Chung was already running downstairs again and beckoning to him. 'Quick! You do all same me tell you, no time for get away now!'

A door was unlocked, Low pushed inside and the door left ajar this time. From under a pallet-bed in the corner Chung dragged a box, from which he took a silk mandarin coat and a wig of blue-black hair, silky smooth and beautifully dressed.

Low was ordered to put them on and lie down on the bed. The noise upstairs grew louder all of a sudden, showing that the police had discovered the trap-door.

Down they came with a rush, a dozen or more of them. Some of them dashed on down the passage, but four or five of them made straight for the open door of Chung Lee's room. But all they saw was a single Chinaman shivering with fright and beseeching them with clasped hands to spare his life and not to wake his wife in bed in the corner.

'Sh! Wifee she sleep, she belly sick, you no wakee!' he begged them, pointing a trembling finger towards her.

They looked across at the bed, seeing only the figure tightly tucked up, the beautifully dressed hair and one silken arm hiding the face. They moved about the room, sounding the walls for hollow spaces, but found none; They looked at the table and saw bills pertaining to onions and a Chinese account book. A moment's silence and then – a few steps nearer would have revealed to the astounded police the face of Craddock Low, that well-known familiar of the police courts, as he stared at the wall with eyes unblinking and sick with terror — but the police moved away and went on down the passage.

An hour later and Low was back among his guests, politely bidding them adieu and commiserating with Mrs Morley on her husband's accident. 'But tell Gordon that all will be well, he needn't worry!' were his last words to her.

Chapter 6

Describing a yacht and a career

THE PRIDE O' MY HEART looked like a beautiful white swan plumed and ready for flight as she lay at her anchorage in Coal Harbor. Her white sides shone dazzlingly in the sun and every bit of brass aboard, down to the remotest nail-head, had been burnished till it reflected the passing clouds above.

She had been built in Hongkong and was lined throughout with teak; in fact, all her fittings and appointments were of a costliness in keeping with the wealth of her owner, Carter McRobbie, who besides being rich by inheritance was the biggest cannery-owner in British Columbia and the possessor of odd lands in unexpected places all over the province.

Just now the owner was entertaining a couple of friends to lunch below, while the skipper and the engineer sat for'ard swinging their heels and chewing the rag. They were due to sail for the north that evening.

'Looks to me as if we're in for a change,' remarked the skipper, spitting deftly overboard. 'Beats me why the boss has left it so late this year. Always known him to go at the first of the month before.'

'Suited me to be down while the *Empress* came in,' said the other, smiling. 'I got the dinkiest bit o' fluff aboard that boat — one o' the stewardesses — say, she's a peach! We knowed each other up in Fort Edward.'

But the skipper was dull of interest in the engineer's love affairs.

'Fort Edward? Was you up there? Why, that's where that guy came from that's lunchin' wi' the boss down there, the guy that's standin' for politics — Gordon Morley's his name.'

'Yep, I seen him come aboard. Same's I seen him step off the boat into Edward first time he lit up there. 'Twas a clean town till he came into it.'

'What d'ye mean?' inquired the skipper, interested at last.

'What I say! 'Twas a decent enough little mining settlement, copper and a sawmill or two, whites and a couple o' dozen chinks to help do the *dirty* work. Then one fine day in blows Gordon Morley from t'other side of hell with a bit o' money in his pocket, and from

that day things changed. He started gambling dens and bad-houses —
financed them himself till they began to pay like smoke; he bought
land, he bought a big share in the mines, and every boat after that
landed *Chinks* — *Chinks* to clear Morley's land, *Chinks* to work
Morley's mines, till Chinatown got bigger than the settlement.'

'But he must have had a pocketful when he went up there, to do
all that!'

'Sure he had! He was a travelling salesman for one o' the Water
Street firms, and some say he made a pile by inventin' the quick way
to get rid of weevils in the cast-off hams. Used to go round to the
outlyin' stores up country and collect all the hams as had gone bad
and crawly, allow the store for 'em, bring 'em back to town, cure
'em of the weevil habit, smoke 'em and sell 'em to the cheap restaurants downtown.'

'Gosh!' said the skipper fervently, and spat again.

'Well, he hadn't been long in Fort Edward afore he got a hold on
the city clerk, and when the little burg got the real estate fever,
believe me, those two they managed so they held back the title
deeds on some excuse so's no one could sell their lots until such time
as the land held by the city clerk and Gordon Morley was cut up in
lots and sold. *Then* the other folk's title deeds was brought out, but
it was mostly too late to sell them, the boom being through!'

'He seems a sweet card, does Gordon,' remarked the skipper, drily.

'Oh, he's sweeter'n that. He took a notion one day he'd like to be
mayor. *Him!* Well, he's got a tongue like milk and honey, and he
made speeches every night sayin' how shameful it was to the credit
of Edward that the town should be so dirty — full of nasty gamblin'
dens an' bad-houses. An' he talked an' he promised that if only the
people'd put him in as mayor he'd make it his duty to clean the
place up. An' moreover, he sent reports of all his speeches to the
Vancouver an' Victoria papers — just to get free publicity.'

'An' did he get in?'

'*You becher life he did*, such was his tongue and such was his
promises. He stayed just long enough to carry 'em out, too; sold his
gamblin' dens, disorderly houses, shares in the mine, saw-mill — *an'
sold 'em to the Chinks.*'

'Hm! Doggone cur!'

'All o' that! I came down in the same boat with him an' his snorty
wife and kid. He'd got himself known down here as the mayor o'

Fort Edward who did what he said an' cleaned up the town, had his face in the papers an' all.'

'An' that's the dog that's goin' to represent us in Parliament, eh? Wonder why the boss is takin' him up, now?'

'Why? Because Politics and Labor walks hand-in-hand, and they're both dependent on the Capitalist, and they none on 'em can do wi'out the Law; that's why the other fellow's here, see?'

And with a grim laugh the engineer gave a hitch to his trousers and went below.

Meanwhile McRobbie and his two guests, Gordon Morley and Craddock Low, were discussing matters that concerned them all over glasses of port and the best cigars.

'If you get in, Gordon, which I hope and expect you will, you'll have to do your level best to try and put your heel on this condemned head tax business. I see they're talking of raising it now. What's to become of employers if they are to be dependent on white labor, eh? Which they mighty soon will be if they do so much to keep yellow labor out!'

Morley leant back and fingered his glass reflectively. His keen eyes seemed to look through his host's face as though they penetrated to the mind itself, then they dropped again to the glass he held.

'You short of Chinese labor up in the cannery, Carter?' he asked casually.

'Short? I should say I was! I'd replace every Indian on the place with a Chinaman, if only I could get them, but there simply aren't enough to be had.'

'And I want them, too, in the worst way,' said Morley. 'You know, I've got some worth-while timber licenses on the island, and I'm just waiting for the number of Chinks I want to start up some sawmills.' Here he glanced across at Low, who acknowledged the glance by dropping his eyes.

'Well,' said the lawyer, after a pause, 'if you both want them as badly as all that, why on earth don't you combine and get 'em out direct from China? Of course you'll have to put up the head tax in a lump sum, but then you can make them repay in work in a very short time. It would pay you!'

McRobbie wondered why the words seemed familiar to him, and then all at once he remembered he had heard words much like them from the mouth of Robert Laidlaw the evening before.

'Well, I'm willing enough,' he exclaimed. 'I'd do almost anything to get them. Should we be 'within the law,' Craddock?' and he laughed a little uneasily. The other two had exchanged satisfied glances.

'Why, sure you would,' replied the lawyer, laughing. 'It's done every day and there's nothing against it, though it's best not to talk too much about it in case white labor should feel aggrieved. But you're not defrauding anybody, and the country must be developed. I don't know where we'd be now if it wasn't for the ubiquitous Chink!'

'Some folk have got their knives into him good and strong,' said McRobbie.

'Have you seen old Laidlaw, of Lulu Island, lately, Carter? He used to be a neighbor of yours, didn't he?'

'Haven't set eyes on him for years. Why, don't he like Chinks, eh?'

'Oh, he says they're a menace to the country, and all the rest of it − "yellow peril," you know, like you read of in story books − but he's mad on the subject, quite mad!'

'Sure he's mad − getting old. Why, the whole blame country 'ud be at a standstill if it wasn't for yellow labor. There'd be no developing it, no trade, nothing. You could never get as much work out of a white man, even if they would work as cheap − which they're not ever likely to, seeing they can't live as cheap. A Chink lives on about five cents a day, and a white man would think he was starving if his food wasn't more than a dollar and a half's worth.'

Morley drained his glass and leaned back, gazing reflectively at the lawyer.

Craddock Low leaned forward with his elbows on the table and smiled at both the others in turn.

'I think,' he said, turning to his host, 'that friend Morley here and I can manage that little deal for you all right. I know an old chap I can trust who'd get us out a bunch of the best straight from China − of his own Tong − and he'd arrange the whole thing for you, for a small commission, of course, and you could pay the head taxes in a lump sum down to him through me. Perfectly simple matter!'

'But,' Morley interrupted, 'they'll be too late over for this season's packing, Carter, I'm afraid, and you'd have to provide them with work from the minute they land. Think you can do that? Of course, I could use my lot straight away — set 'em lumbering any old time of year.'

McRobbie didn't answer all at once. He was turning things over in his mind. He lit his pipe slowly. Certain words he had heard yesterday came back to him: 'They're creeping into everything ... slowly but surely, beating us at our own game ... it's up to such as you to save your country for your own nation — let alone your own race.' But, damn it all, the old fool was mad, in his second childhood; he had already lived too long, ruining two lives with his cursed old age — and again a wave of bitterness overwhelmed the voice of conscience.

'Sure, I could use them,' he said, bringing his fist down on the table. 'I've got a 2,000-acre bit of first-class land in the Lillooet district which I can't use till it's irrigated. I'd set 'em to clearing that. Done with you, Craddock. You arrange that for me and let me know what I owe you.'

The lawyer waved his hand as though to banish such sordid trifles as mere money from the conversation, and intimated that he was only too glad to feel he had been of some small service to a friend who wanted help in developing the industries of the country.

He didn't think it worth while to mention the fact that he had been instrumental in the same importation of Chinese for half a dozen other employers.

'We'll have another drink on the bargain,' said McRobbie, filling up their glasses.

And so it came about that between two and three hundred Chinese coolies were brought into the country by Chung Lee through Craddock Low at the bidding of Morley and McRobbie.

And the coolies in turn brought their various wives and other little fancies who were not wives, and they all flourished and multiplied exceedingly.

The sun was a fiery red ball just sinking behind the Island mountains when the *Pride o' My Heart* sped swiftly over a glassy sea out through the Narrows, leaving a frothy white V in her wake.

The skipper was at the wheel, happy once more. He hated dawdling about on shore, and he couldn't think why — but it was none of his business to wonder why they put to sea so late any more than it was to know why the boss hung round Vancouver when he might be and ought to be up north watching his interests in the cannery.

The boss himself was standing astern watching the fast retreating shores of Stanley Park, a lonely figure outlined against the dim, dark evening sky.

The difficulties that assailed him as an employer of labor in a big way were overcome. The path had been made easy for him – in fact, the skids were greased – and yet ... The problem of labor ashore had been solved in a very simple way through an unexpected source; the other problem of labor afloat, i.e., more fishermen to bring in a heavier stream of the unlimited salmon that were there to be caught for the asking, he had hoped was also solved.

At the head of the few Jap fishermen who were already working for him so satisfactorily up at Rivers Inlet and around was a jolly little brown man with twinkling eyes and a beaming smile called Hoshimura, and it was this very man that had proposed to him a plan – a plan so daring, so seemingly unfeasible but withal so simple if successful that McRobbie had laughed at it.

But Hoshimura held a stout and unwavering faith in the courage and endurance of his fellow-countrymen and talked so convincingly that McRobbie gave him a free hand to try and work out his plan, promising him what he liked in the uncertain event of his success in landing such large numbers of his 'cousins' without the knowledge or interference of the Government authorities.

It was a great pity that the Government had made immigration laws necessitating such foxy measures. Three years ago the Post-master-General had run over to Japan in a friendly way to arrange about restricting (also in a friendly way) the immigration of Japs into Canada, which was becoming such as to worry certain ranting old busybodies like Laidlaw, for instance, who had no personal interest in the problem of labor.

So the immigrants from the land of almond blossoms and chrysanthemums were thereupon limited to a paltry 400 a year, and the Government was still very strict in its watch.*

McRobbie had agreed with Hoshimura that it would be a good deal better in every way for him, McRobbie, to be as far away as

---

*This number has never been adhered to and has increased steadily ever since. In 1918-19 no less than 1,178 Japs entered Canada; since July 1, 1900, the total number of Japs entering has been 19,886. (This is up to July 1920).

possible during the arrival of the contraband Japs, so that he might say with truth that he knew nothing whatever about it — might easily refuse to believe it possible, in fact.

So he stood there, smoking, alone with his thoughts, and while he watched the fast-receding shores growing ever dimmer with distance and darkness till they became vague and shadowy as the land of might-have-been, he visualized anew the face and form of the woman he loved.

Twelve years since life became to him a valueless, empty thing without her — since he had first asked her to marry him. For twelve years he had been trying to get rid of his heart, doing his honest best to take her advice and put another woman in the place that duty forbade this one to fill. But ever at the crucial moment her face would come up in mind and heart, wholesome, sweet, beloved. How long must he wait before death swept away that insuperable obstacle — that ranting old fanatic who had already done his day's work and was now less help than hindrance here on earth?

With exceeding bitterness filling his soul Carter McRobbie turned on his heel and went below.

Chapter 7

In which the fish inspector sees something that makes him sit up

AWAY UP NORTH on the coastwise side of Hunter Island and opposite to the opening of that labyrinth of inland seas called Burke Channel there is a little bay sheltered from three winds and passing beautiful. There is a stretch of yellow sand which at low water shows the tracks of herons and seagulls, of an occasional deer or wandering coon, but seldom, very seldom, does it bear the imprint of man.

On either side of it tall, ragged Douglas firs and hemlock grow right down to the water's edge, reduplicating their height, when the shadows grow long, in the glass-smooth sea. There are big boulders whereon flap lazy seals, shiny and wet and glistening, ready to slide down into the water again at a moment's notice should anything disturb them — but nothing ever comes. There is never any sound but the gurgle of the butterballs calling to each other across the bay, the flat, comfortable quacking of duck, the honk of a flight of geese above the monotonous wash of little waves that vainly froth and fume up the sand waiting for the feet of little children that never come.

Here it was that the dawn of a certain day found a big, white gasoline launch at anchorage, the Government fishery boat, and the Fisheries Inspector, J.B. Harding, was aboard.

It was so early that the tips of the distant snow peaks on the mainland coast were still rosy with the flush of the rising sun, but aboard the *Hawk* everyone was awake and hurrying about his business. A man on deck was rubbing up the brasswork, another was cleaning the engine, and the man bending diligently over the pan of bacon sizzling on the stove was no less a person than J.B. Harding himself, who was very particular as to how his bacon was cooked.

Presently the aromatic fumes of coffee mingled agreeably with the smell of smoked bacon (causing the saliva to drip sadly from the jowl of a black bear ambling vaguely through the woods a mile away), and the crew of the *Hawk* sat down to an early breakfast. It had to be early, for they wanted to make Bella Bella before the heat of the day came on; the weather was all too sultry just now not to be somewhere in the shade during the noon hours.

Within the hour all was ready for the anchor. The engine began to sing and the boat got under way; the little divers that had been pluming themselves so peacefully on the water fled from under her bows, screeching indignant surprise with a great fluster and scurry of wings. Very soon the bay was left behind to dream on undisturbed for another season or so. The *Hawk* turned her nose northwards and steamed up coast for a mile or so, but here she slowed down again. There was a bit of a river hereabouts just big enough to be charted.

The dinghy was hauled in and two men, Harding and another, put ashore for a double purpose. They wanted to get water and they wanted to make sure that no one was fishing the mouth of this river without a license. But there was no sign of life on land or afloat as they neared the shore, only the splash now and then of a leaping salmon and the dazzling glisten of its silver body as it caught the sun in mid-air. The Inspector grunted to himself. 'Darned sight too many fish jumping round to be natural,' he said.

'Shall I beach her here?' asked the man who was rowing, indicating a spot to one side of the river's mouth.

'No; go straight on up the mouth and beach her on that bit of shingle under the bank,' the Inspector replied. He had been too long in the service not to do his work thoroughly. As they rowed on slowly he seemed to be sharply on the watch for something on either side of him.

'Slowly, Tom, slowly,' he said with his eyes searching the water. 'Look down here!' They both leaned overboard. The water just here was not over-clear, but at a yard or so's depth it was alive with fish — salmon.

The Inspector's eyes shifted to the bank again, and all of a sudden something caught his attention. It was to all appearances a smooth, brown stone about the size of a cricket ball, and certainly indistinguishable save to one who was looking for it. But it was not a stone, for it bobbed up and down in the water.

An exclamation broke from the lips of Harding as he saw it, and immediately he turned to look at the other side of the mouth to find its fellow.

'*See that, Tom? And that?*' he cried, pointing triumphantly at the little brown balls bobbing about on either side. 'Now *go slow* and you'll see what you will see.'

But something appeared to be obstructing the nose of the boat and Tom's efforts made but little headway. Gradually, however, they moved on, and just as gradually the little cork floats on either side closed in behind them as the net they held was carried onwards by the boat's nose.

'Just as I thought,' called out the Inspector, triumphantly. '*Those damned Japs again* – and they haven't even got a drag-seine license for this place!' They began to haul the net into the boat.

At this season of the year the salmon return to the rivers whence they sprung in order to spawn, so that a favorite place for a drag-seine net is in the bay to one side of the mouth of a river, where the fish are bound to gather in large numbers, and the net can be worked from the beach in a circle and dragged ashore.

But the Japs, in their greed and anxiety to get what they can while the getting's good – they need take no thought for the morrow in another man's hunting-grounds – are apt to go one better. They close up the whole mouth of the river with a net, leave it so for several days, then come back to make a clean haul of *all* the fish gathered there, waiting in vain to return to their spawning grounds – for a salmon will never return to any but its own particular river to spawn. In this way only a negligible percentage of salmon are able to spawn, and so the apparently unlimited stock of pink and silver fish that form the second greatest industry of British Columbia runs low, and in time will run out, just as the buffalo, that were at one time considered limitless, have in a comparatively few years become extinct.

Well satisfied with his morning's work, Harding and his men turned northwards again, hugging the shores of Hunter Island and keeping a close lookout for a dirty little chug-chug boat that might belong to the miscreant Japs, though with little hope of finding them.

The sun was high in the heavens and already beating mercilessly down on a shadeless sea when the *Hawk* rounded the northernmost point of Hunter Island and turned westward along the shores of Denny Island, heading for Bella Bella.

Harding himself was stretched at full length on deck in the bows with his back against the deck-house, a pencil and note-book in his hand; he was ostensibly making up his papers, but his fedora hat was tilted over his eyes, and truth to tell he was very nearly asleep.

It was the blackfish that startled him into wakefulness again. Someone astern shouted out *'Blackfish ahoy!'* and Harding sat up to see a school of them rolling along, heaving their gigantic forms in and out of sight between the boat and the shore, far too near to be pleasant. The *Hawk* moved out of her course a little so as to avoid any laggards there might be following the main school, and to do this she headed for a minute or so due west, so that Harding found himself looking straight through the channel between Hunter and Campbell Islands – straight out to the open Pacific beyond.

And as he looked he saw – or thought he saw – something that made him rub those keen grey eyes of his and sit bolt upright to look again. Then he got up and made his way astern to fetch his glasses; he looked again through those and then passed them on to the next man. 'Tell me what you see out there, Tom!'

'Why, it looks to me like a kind of a *sail*, but I never seen a sail that big or that shape, not in all *my* born days!'

Each man looked in turn and each was more puzzled than the last.

'Maybe it's only a cloud,' said one, but the others were agreed it was too concrete a thing for a cloud.

'Well, it don't seem to be making much headway, whatever it is, and that's just about what a sail would do, seeing there ain't no sort o' wind.' 'Gosh darn it!' said another. 'What kind o' booby suckers are we all? Why, it's a *mirage*, that's what it is!'

But no, the others would not agree that it was a mirage – which, all the same, are very common in these parts – and presently the shores of Campbell Island intervened and the channel was out of sight. Harding alone was still puzzling in his mind as to the identity of the mystery.

Past Denny Island they came and on up to the wharf at Bella Bella.

Peter McReady, the storekeeper at Bella Bella, was an old friend of J.B. Harding's. He was a toughish-looking, middle-aged man with stubby red beard and a hearty laugh that was known and welcomed by all seafaring men between Nome and Seattle. He had marked the coming of the Government boat from afar and was standing on the verandah of his store ready with a greeting for Harding, in blue overalls that barely covered his portly frame, and the usual little bag of Old Chum dangling from his waist-line.

It was just about the luncheon hour and there were several small groups of men sitting about in twos and threes in any shade they could find. It was very hot. Inside the store there were the usual cluster of men lolling over their glasses on the counter, but Peter McReady and Harding passed straight through to the little room behind.

'Must eat sometime, I guess, and better now than never,' the store-keeper remarked as he threw a few sticks into the stove and put a light to them, and set the kettle on for tea.

Harding quite agreed with him. They exchanged the latest gossip concerning coasting boats and people who were wont to pass that way, during which the storekeeper busied himself with preparations for a meal. He opened a tin of corned beef and another of pineapple, set a bottle of tomato ketchup, a hunk of cheese and a billycan of tea on the table.

'We should have been up earlier if we hadn't been kept by that blamed block-net of the Japs across that river,' Harding was saying. 'Have you any kind of idea, Pete, who they might be?'

'I guess it'd be like looking for a needle in a haystack; they be just as thick as flies around these parts, as you know. They might be ones from that cannery of their own up at Jackson Pass, and then again they might be from any of the other canneries. Believe me, 'twas a sorry day for the fish you Government chaps ever let Japs in on this game. It's their natural life, fishin'; they're born to it, an' the cheap way they live the white men don't have a look in!'

'You don't need to tell me, Pete; I know. But what can you do? The cannery-owners *will* have them, tumble over each other to get them, and the way they fish — well, there won't be half a salmon left in BC waters in a few years' time!'

'Well, ain't there no law to forbid 'em comin' in, same as there's a head tax on the Chink?'

'Only a sort of friendly agreement we had with Japan three years ago to limit them coming in above 400 a year. But, man alive,' and here the Inspector leaned over and thumped the table with his fist, 'these doggone rich cannery-men wouldn't stop at that! They'd *stop at nothing to get 'em in* — can't afford *not* to have 'em these days, they say.'

It was not until the meal was over and they had lit up that Harding remembered to mention the mysterious sail that had puzzled them all outside Queen's Sound. It puzzled Peter McReady, too. He knit his brows over it.

'Bigger'n any sail you ever seen,' he repeated, 'an' a different shape and seemingly makin' no headway? It fair gets me! Why, it'd be 'way out o' the line of all the fishin' except the halibut, an' a-course they're all steam now.!'

'Jake said it was a mirage.'

But Pete shook his head. 'Nope, that warn't no mirage, neither,' and he puffed away at his pipe, thinking deeply. Suddenly he leaned forward, looking hard at the other man. '*By gosh!*' he muttered, in a husky whisper.

'Well?' asked Harding, patiently waiting to hear the result of this brainwave. But a question came instead.

'You goin' to look in at the Jap cannery at Jackson Pass tomorrow?'

'Sure, we'll make it to night, I think. But what's that got to do with it?'

'Well, look in here on your way back,' replied Pete, and that is all he would say about it — not another word.

Chapter 8

In which Harding comes upon a 'pleasant joke'

THE HAWK MADE good time that afternoon going north past the Bardswell Islands, out into the open sea at Milbank Sound, then up another channel, making straight for the Japanese cannery at Jackson Pass. It was fairly late when the anchor went overboard, and the glooming mountains round sent ever-lengthening, sombre shadows into the oily water below. The inlet was dotted with the grimy little gasoline launches of the Japs and the still evening air re-echoed with the throbbing of the chug-chug engines of homing fishermen.

'Going ashore now or will we have supper first?' one of the men asked Harding.

'No; I've a notion to take the dinghy and row round the point. There's a creek behind there that I want to examine before it gets too dark. Come on, Tom! We'll be back by the time you get supper ready.'

So they made for the point where a screen of tall firs stood out black as ink against the evening sky and photographed themselves again in the water. The gentle 'splash, splash' of their oars and the creak of the row-locks hardly disturbed a sheldrake and his ducks dozing happily as they drifted along on the tide under the point.

Tom was standing up and rowing forward after the fashion of the Pacific Coast, so that both men had their eyes afront as they rounded the point. One stood up in his excitement and the other nearly dropped the oars in his astonishment at the sight that met their eyes.

A gigantic sail of a shape and size unknown to British Columbia rose apparently straight out of the water before them.

'*By gosh! What the hell's that?*' said Tom, in a suppressed undertone, as though he gazed on an apparition from another world. Another look revealed the fact that the sail rose from a curiously shaped boat with a square stern and a curved roof over the body of it.

'*That's a Japanese sampan*,' said Harding, grimly, 'and I'd like to know what the devil it's doing here! And that – *that*, Tom, is the *same sail as what we saw outside Queen's Sound!*'

'I'm thinking it sure is,' said Tom, nodding solemnly.

As they rowed nearer they saw that the boat was alive with little brown men swarming about it like busy ants, that it was moored to the rocks ashore, that several little gasoline launches were drawn up alongside.

It was nearly dusk when they too drew up alongside the sampan and shipped their oars. Harding hailed a Jap who seemed to be in charge and directing the others. He came running towards them at once, threading his way between the barrels and wooden boxes with which the boat was scattered. He grinned and bowed to the two white men.

'Where did this come from?' Harding asked him shortly.

'Honorable Mister, we make it hereabouts like pleasant joke for to sail in Sound and make think we are like home, see?

Harding and his companion looked at each other and laughed. It struck them both that it was a very un-Japlike proceeding to spend so much time building an enormous sampan merely for a 'pleasant joke.' The little Jap laughed, too – doubled himself up with laughing.

'Where did you build it?' Harding asked again, sternly.

The Jap shrugged his shoulders and waved his arms to indicate the forest-clad mountains round him.

'Much honorable trees hereabout, mister, much pleasing hard work, yes?' and he laughed again.

Tom was examining closely the rust-colored wood, so well oiled and weatherproof, of which the boat was made.

'*This ain't no BC timber*,' he was saying, and he whipped out a knife and scraped the side a little the better to examine it.

It was almost too dark to see the grain of the lumber, but they both came to the conclusion that it was of no tree grown in British Columbia. By that time it was so dark that nothing remained but to give up the inspection and return to the *Hawk*.

That night Harding went ashore to interview Yamato, the suave and superlatively polite owner of the Japanese cannery. Concerning the sampan, he also seemed to regard it as a childish frolic of those of his men who found time hanging heavily on their hands, and laughed as merrily as the other had done at the idea of Harding viewing it as anything but a joke – a plaything, so to speak.

But Harding was puzzled. The idea of a Jap with time on his hands to spare for anything not actually profitable was just ridiculous.

'They seem pretty seaworthy, anyway,' the Inspector remarked drily. 'Where were the ones we saw out to sea when we were passing Queen's Sound bound for?'

Yamato laughed again, but Harding thought he detected a gleam of something that wasn't laughter in the little black eyes.

'Them coming from Queen Charlotte Island, honorable mister,' was the reply.

'I see. You've got a stake up there, too, haven't you? And where were they going to?'

'Them coming here only honorable wind blowing them away far, too much pity, yes?'

Harding scratched his head thoughtfully. But there was no further information to be got out of Yamato anent this surprising fleet of 'pleasant jokes,' so he went ahead with the ordinary routine of his inspection.

It was not long after sun-up next morning when Harding and one of his men rowed round the point to make a closer inspection of the sampan by the clear light of day. But no sooner had they rounded the point than they realized that they were too late; *there was no trace of the sampan to be seen.* They rowed up to the place where it had been moored the night before, but it was as if it had never been.

'Now the question is,' said Harding, 'did they sail out last night, or have they destroyed it?'

'No wind last night,' his companion answered, 'and they'd have took three or four gas-boats to tow out a thing like that, and we don't sleep so heavy as we wouldn't ha' heard that many passing close to us and all at once.'

'You're right, Tom, I guess. Then they must have destroyed it, and they must have worked like blame niggers to do it in the time.'

They questioned some Japs working at their nets on the further shore.

'She making no good,' was the answer they received. 'We chopping she up in little bits for making fire, honorable mister.'

And that was all they could find out about the apparition of the night before.

'That warn't *no BC-grown timber* as that there sampan was built of,' Tom said more than once as they rowed slowly back to the *Hawk.* 'I'd swear in my grave to that.'

And Harding agreed with him, but the fact complicated the

puzzle. There could only be one possible solution to it all, but Harding put it from him as impossible.

It was Peter McReady who laughed at his doubts when they got back to Bella Bella. He smacked his thigh and guffawed with a heartiness that brought a smile to the lips of the men sitting with their drinks on upturned boxes about the store.

'*Believe me, John, that's sure what they done,*,' he said, leaning over the counter and addressing himself to Harding. 'They've come 'way over the Pacific in their doggone sampans, right straight into the arms of the cannery men waiting wide open to welcome them.'

Harding, his pipe between his teeth, leaned back against the counter, his arms folded and his eyes fixed frowning on the floor. There was a murmur of unbelief amongst the others.

'Oh, snakes!' said one. 'It's a darned sight easier to believe they made 'em on the spot, same's they told you.'

But the Inspector shook his head. 'No,' he replied, slowly, 'I only wish we could believe that, but they weren't made out of any timber that grows on this side of the ocean, we could both swear to that.'

'Tain't so impossible, neither,' put in Pete. 'Them sampans are built to stand any kind o' sea, as I've heard tell, and the Japs is a seagoin' nation, and with the promises held out to them on this side by them as wants them – well, why wouldn't they risk a bit?'

'Well, what's the idee, anyway?' asked another, 'o' riskin' a bug-house voyage like that one, when they could come into the country in the ornery way – in their own boats if they like? They ain't got no head tax on 'em like the Chinks has.'

'Why, because the Government won't *let* 'em in beyond a certain number – that's the only protection we got agin 'em, and that's not sayin' much neither, 'cos them as wants 'em will pay anything to git 'em, and the Government bein' human 'ud rather shut its eyes than its pockets.'

'Well,' put in a bluff old fisherman, 'I'll say this, the more o' these gol-darned Japs we have the less fish we catch. They're a blessed sight too clever at this game, an' they don't care a tincan what comes o' the fish tomorrow so's they catch it today. An' what's more, if we keep on lettin' 'em in at the rate they're comin' in, in a few more years there won't be any more salmon for us to catch, speshly sockeye.'

'You're right there,' said Harding, shortly, nodding to the speaker, 'there won't.'

'Well, what for do they want to leave their own blame country, anyway?' cried another.

'Why? *Because they're increasing like the vermin they are*,' replied Pete, thumping his fist on the counter. 'I read in a book they're multiplyin' themselves at the rate of 400,000 a year, and their population's already 350 per square mile, where it's only 25 in Canada. *What do you know 'bout that?* Small blame to them they want another country to overflow theirselves into, and why wouldn't this be the nat'ral one? Same climate, same industries, same conditions!'

'Let the Japs stick to Asia,' said Harding. 'This is a white man's country. We can't mix with them – that is, they can't become Canadians, not in a thousand years, so they best keep out.'

'What were the idee, anyway, o' makin' you think they was makin' them sampans up in Queen Charlotte Island?'

'Well, they got a good big stake up there in Lasquito Harbor – gold mine. Ain't that so?'

'Yes,' Harding replied, 'there's a regular Japtown up there, they tell me, though I never been there to see, myself. They don't slip much gold out to us, anyway.'

Peter McReady leaned still further across the counter.

'And is our Government asleep that they don't see what's goin' on under their nose?' he asked. 'What d'you s'pose them Japs wants with owning land that's the *westernmost point on the coast of BC*?'

'What d'you mean, Pete?'

The man's voice dropped to a husky but none the less impressive whisper.

'*Meanin' it's the first and most convenient point that a fleet would be like to touch at comin' across the seas straight from t'other side!*'

They didn't quite catch his meaning even then.

'Fleet? What fleet?' they asked, stupidly.

'Fleet o' ships – battleships – nasty-lookin' kind o' ships when they aren't friendly – *Jap ships*, boys. An' it would come mighty convenient for them to have a friendly station at the first point they touches!'

The others took this idea variously. Harding refilled his pipe, with his eyes on Pete, puzzled and disturbed.

'By gosh!' exclaimed one, 'you been doin' some thinkin', Pete. War with Japan! Snakes! That'll never come!'

'Never's a long day, and when one country's too sleepy to see another comin' in in fishin' boats, they sure won't wake up in time to see 'em comin' over in warships.'

Chapter 9

In which Harding finds that two and two make four

THE COASTWISE PASSENGER boat that called at Bella Bella next day took down a carefully sealed and urgent letter from the Fisheries Inspector to the customs authorities at Victoria, telling of the incident of the sampans and urging that the matter be looked into without delay.

The Government, to its credit, lost no time in sending one of their two light cruisers up north to see what they could see, but they came back with nothing to report, which was not surprising considering that all trace of the sampans had been done away with or hidden long before the cruiser had put out from Victoria. So the incident was put on one side and forgotten — if not actually disbelieved — by all save Harding, who had come up against it.

The day after they left Bella Bella the *Hawk* was chugging busily up Rivers Inlet and Harding saw with a sense of satisfaction that the luxurious private yacht, *Pride o' My Heart*, belonging to the wealthy cannery man, Carter McRobbie, was at her moorings in front of the big cannery.

Many were the excellent little lunches and dinners of which he had partaken on board the yacht during his periodical visits of inspection, and he had always carried away pleasing memories of a thoroughly genial host.

This time, however, he was destined to be disappointed. Mr McRobbie was ashore and appeared to be in so much of a hurry over something or other that he could not spare time for more than a very cursory welcome to the Fisheries Inspector. The latter was turned over to the manager of the cannery in the most businesslike way possible, so that no time at all was left for asking the most ordinary questions as to catches and runs and hands and so on. In fact, it almost seemed to Harding that McRobbie ran away down to his dinghy — ran away from possible questions.

However, that was neither here nor there, after all, and the Inspector shrugged his shoulders and got to business with the manager as to the exact tallying of licenses issued with hands employed, and details about nets. The cannery seemed particularly prosperous, with a myriad little gas launches coming and going and buzzing about like May-flies on a summer morning. It was a cosmopolitan place, too, with all those Chinese packers working side by side with Indian klootches ashore, and afloat Indians, white men — amongst whom were Swedes, Norwegians, hard-bitten Americans, Canadians from the east, Finlanders, Austrians, Danes, even an Icelander or two — and Japs; yes, there certainly were more Japs than any.

And as he noticed this Harding began to wonder, and as he wondered he added two and two. He did not see McRobbie again, for when he had finished his tour of inspection the *Pride o' My Heart* was no more to be seen — she had slipped her moorings and gone off on a cruise, he had been told. It was strangely inconsistent with the owner's former receptions of him. Could it be that McRobbie was trying to avoid him? And if so, why? What has he to hide?

The number of Japs fishing? How was it that he, Harding, had never been struck by this before at his cannery? If the sampan that he had seen outside Queen's Sound had kept on her course she would have fetched up exactly at Rivers Inlet. Two and two made four, and Harding began to ask himself whether it could be possible for a man like McRobbie to be so far in league with the Japs as to descend to hood-winking his own Government in order to get them into the country for his own especial benefit.

He pondered the question far into the night and came to no satisfactory solution of it when at last he shook out his pipe with a sigh and turned in.

Meanwhile the unconscious object of his speculations, McRobbie, and the man in charge of his Jap fishing fleet, one Hoshimura aforementioned, were heartily congratulating themselves on success-fully outwitting the all too keen wits of the Fisheries Inspector. The extra odd hundred or so fellow-countrymen of Hoshimura's that they had acquired to swell their fleet within the last two days would have been a little difficult to account for had the Inspector proved unduly inquisitive.

Hoshimura was further congratulating himself on signal service rendered to his country. Every man that landed on the coast and gained a foothold on this side of the ocean was an anchorage that turned a strange land into a potential colony and bound it with steel chains to the little Mother-empire across the seas. But he did not communicate these thoughts to McRobbie.

Hoshimura's family was doing well in the service of the Empire. Some of his 'cousins' (it is wonderful to hear of the overwhelming numbers of cousinly relatives possessed by both the Chinese and the Japanese) had bought up timber licenses and were working lumber mills on their own; others had mines, gold, copper, coal, sulphur and other things; they were edging their way deep into the fish industry, they were even beginning to exploit their own natural industry, gardening, and two of his relatives had bought land in the Mission district, in the valley of the Fraser River, the heart of the best small-fruit country in British Columbia.

True, they were not yet so strong as they were on the other side of the line, in California and Washington, where they owned some of the biggest hotels — but the day would come. Patience, perseverance and hard work would win the day. A great fact in their favor was that the white man had an objection to living next to a Jap — even with a fence between. Strange, but it was so. Thus these fastidious whites played into their hands.

They found that whenever a Jap bought a plot of land the white man next to him moved out. So the obvious idea was, not to centralize like the stupid Chinese, but buy here and there, at either end of a road, for instance, and when the white neighbors moved out, immediately to buy up the vacant plots, and so gradually close in little by little, year by year, until the two or three whites left in the centre plots found themselves surrounded by a colony of Japs and moved out in self-defence.

Hoshimura, Yamato and several other influential Japs had for several years watched the working of this plan and found it so simple and so successful that they had advised the home government to lend money on it. Loans for the purpose of acquiring land in a systematic way overseas were promptly forthcoming, at a low rate of interest, and little nucleus Jap colonies had sprung up all over British Columbia, not quite so indiscriminately scattered about in odd and useless corners as one might suppose. The Japanese have not changed what was a tourist's dream of almond blossoms and chrysanthemums into a first-class Power in fifty years by employing indiscriminate methods. They are far too clever for that.

One other incident served to strengthen the impression that had lain dormant until the last few days in Harding's mind — the impression of *systematic purpose among the Japanese towards some definite end.* It was on the following evening that the *Hawk* was ploughing her peaceful way over the waters of an obscure inlet into which flowed several small creeks that needed inspection. Here were no fishing launches to be seen; in fact, the only sign of civilization was a shingle mill that looked as though it had been thrown onto the side of the mountain that came sheer down into the sea.

As they sped up the inlet they passed a little rowing boat with a single man in it bending diligently over his oars, and he was a Jap. It was late in the evening, so the monotonous rasp of the saw at the mill was hushed, and as they tied up for the night at the floating wharf below the mill the voices of men above sitting and talking over their evening pipe re-echoed from side to side among the mountains.

The manager came out and hailed Harding, cordially inviting him and the other two to come ashore and have a feed in the cookhouse. Any arrival was an event in the camp, particularly one that was outside the usual routine of visitors. So the passengers of the *Hawk* accepted the invitation and went ashore, accompanying the genial manager to the cook-house.

'We'se all done finished eatin',' the host explained, 'but the cook'll put you up a dinky feed afore you can sneeze!' They passed through the eating-room, with its long, white oilcloth-covered tables, into the kitchen beyond, but this also was deserted.

'*Gosh darn it!* Where'd the son-of-a-gun be now!' said mine host, banging at the door of the cook's quarters. But no answer was forthcoming.

'Never seed such a guy for boatin' as this yer cook be. D'recly the minute he washed up an' finished off he goes with his lil' old boat 'way up the inlet and down the inlet an' everywhere. An' 'taint because he's fishin' all the time; it's on'y 'bout once in a while he'll bring back fish.'

'Is he a Jap?' asked Harding. 'Because if so we passed him 'way down the coast.'

'That's him, for sure. That's Shimadzu. Say, now, what'll we do?' But the perturbed host was assured that the visitors were not so hungry that they could not wait until the cook returned, and meanwhile they would enjoy 'swapping lies' with the longshoremen.

In due course the crew of the *Hawk* were sitting down to the pinkest of pink hams, a piled-up dish of fried eggs, blueberry pie, succulent fresh rolls, and coffee that tasted as fragrant as it smelt.

The little Jap cook waited on their needs with a beaming smile and a joyful chuckle that made it a matter of impossibility for anyone to find fault with or even demur at his absence.

After the meal was over Harding went for a stroll with the manager. They walked up to look at a lake at some little distance from the camp, a lake so stiff with trout that it was, the men said, no fun at all to catch them; and moreover, it had no visible outlet and no streams to feed it. Harding was interested and they stayed talking till after dark.

When they returned the camp was in darkness save for a dim light in the bunk-house and another in the cook's quarters in the cook-house. As they passed this latter the manager remarked that it was no unusual thing for the cook to burn his midnight oil far into the small hours, but whether he read or whether he worked no one knew.

Some instinctive force impelled Harding to step aside and look in at that lighted window. He saw a sight that remained with him always and returned in after years like a photograph to remind him of a warning that he might have taken more seriously than he did and so have helped to avert the deluge that came after.

The little cook was sitting at one end of a table, which was spread all over with charts, maps and papers covered with calculations. But he was no longer smiling; he was frowning, and by the light of a hurricane-lamp hanging over him he was moving a compass and a ruler on a chart and referring every now and then to his figures. That they were maps and charts of the British Columbia coast Harding could see; he also saw that they were of such detail of every nook and cranny, of inlet and headland, as he had never seen among any of the stocks of Government charts.

And as he gazed on the sight in wonder, Shimadzu, the Jap, looked up and saw him, and instead of the jolly smile there came over his face a look of intense, malignant hatred, and into his eyes a gleam of sly malice. Harding remembered that look years afterwards.

Chapter 10

In which Mrs Morley attends a reception

THE ELECTIONS, with all their excitement, were over and forgotten. That Gordon Morley had been returned with a big majority as one of the members for Vancouver was no surprise to any who knew the man, least of all to his wife. Her delight, however, was none the less, and she basked in the reflected glory of his increased importance like a cat in the hot sunshine.

The placards that had become familiar upon hoardings all over Vancouver, beseeching the public to vote for Gordon Morley, the 'people's friend,' and showing below the list of planks that were to be the aims and ideals of his public service, were not pasted over with advertisements for canned milk and future concerts. And this was just as well, for of them all only one was in the way of being carried into force as a result of his promises.

This was *'Good Roads for Farmers,'* and the sum of money that Morley had persuaded his party to vote for this purpose sounded good and practical in the ears of those worthy British Columbians who favored agricultural progress. Except a very few on the spot who took the trouble to inquire into the matter, no one could know that ninety per cent of the particular farmers who were to benefit directly from these initial roads were Chinamen, and still less did these few guess even remotely at the substantial little sum that found its way through the agency of a certain old reprobate, Chung Lee, from the pockets of the up-country Chinamen into the bank account of Gordon Morley.

The contractor for these roads was, of course, that same George Worrall who had had it in his power to command a certain number of votes for Morley. So it was all worked — on the principle of the old rhyme:

Big fleas have little fleas upon their backs to bite 'em,
And little fleas have lesser fleas, and so ad infinitum.

As to the second plank regarding the North Vancouver bridge across the Second Narrows, the credulity of those unhappy owners of lots on the prospective site was such that every cause but the right one was blamed for the failure of the bridge idea. The slump had already set in, the dominion government engineer was blamed for his laggard policy in refusing to sanction the proposal of the bridge, and the newspapers, preferring to uphold the provincial government, printed long and sympathetic accounts of Gordon Morley's pluck in fighting to the bitter end the lost battle of the bridge with the dominion government.

In nine days' time both the battle and the bridge were forgotten, and public interest, in a country where fortunes are made and lost in less time than it takes to write about them, was turned toward the next speculation. Somehow or other Gordon Morley escaped all shadow of condemnation, and if anybody but his wife ever suspected that he had made a fortune out of the 'lost battle of the bridge' nobody let the cat out of the bag. For one reason, he was a man who made a vastly unpleasant enemy.

If his wife had her suspicions, they rather had the effect of deepening her admiration for his cunning. She knew she had lost the $300-odd that she put into her North Shore lots, but she had in its place suddenly gained a good and solid bank account of her very own that ran into little short of five figures.

It was nothing to her and it was less to her husband that hundreds of people had sold all their securities and plunged heavily on the strength of Morley's promises; that many a hardworking stenographer had withdrawn all her savings of years in order to buy a lot she had never seen because she also believed in Morley; and that all these people had exchanged good money for worthless paper because the land they had burdened themselves with might only with luck be sold within a century for perhaps one-tenth of the money paid for it.

Rose Morley cared for nothing but the present concrete and highly satisfactory fact that she and Bobbie were staying at the Empress Hotel in Victoria with her husband, who was an MP and able to write 'Honorable' before his name during such time as Parliament sat and his duties required him to reside in the capital.

Bobbie had been put to school in Victoria as a day-boy, not, as his mother urged, as a boarder until his parents had to leave the town. Meanwhile his father insisted that the boy should spend as much of his time with them as possible, and little Bobbie, in whose eyes there were no other gods but his father, was nothing loth.

Rose left the two to spend their off-hours together as they wished. She herself found her days full and very pleasant. Her new position entitled her to many invitations and acquaintances that she had never dared to hope for, and on the day she received a card for a reception at old Mrs McRobbie's new and palatial residence her cup of happiness was full.

Her husband found time to drive her himself to the gates of the mighty, and she descended at the door in all the glory of white kid gloves and a new silk dress whose rustling barely concealed the creaking of stays drawn so tight that their owner could scarcely breathe, much less bend.

Mrs McRobbie, an old lady with no nonsense about her, and fine white hair, received her guests with a welcome that made acquaintances feel like lifelong friends. Mrs Morley was given plenty of opportunity to purr her ecstatic approval of the new house into her hostess's ears.

She praised the curtains and admired the carpets; she fell into ecstasies over the lavish arrangements of flowers, and declared that the artistic choice of old English pieces of furniture was an education in itself.

'Yes, yes, I know it's pretty,' agreed Mrs McRobbie. 'It's just the prettiest and most convenient home I've ever had, but I'd a deal sooner the boy had built it for a young wife. I'd be happy enough myself in a small, wee house, watching the two young ones making a home of this.' She shook her head sadly.

'So you'd be glad to see your son married, Mrs. McRobbie?' asked Mrs Morley, with some surprise. 'Well, it sure does seem strange that he's stayed single so long, and him as handsome as paint and all. But p'raps he has someone in his mind's eye. You never know!'

'Not that *I've* ever heard of, and he knows how glad for him I'd be over it!'

'Is he in Victoria now during the session?' Mrs Morley privately thought she was asking rather a superfluous question, as to her new way of thinking nobody who was anybody would care to confess that they were not necessarily connected with Parliament. But to her surprise Mrs McRobbie denied it.

'Oh, no; he's always up at Rivers Inlet this time of the year, like his father was before him. He was late going up this time, so likely won't be down before the end of the season. And then,' she added, 'we are going to the Old Country for a trip.'

'My, how fine! I must try and persuade Gordon to take me on a tour sometime when Parliament can spare him, you know, but that won't be just yet. I guess you have plenty of friends in the Old Country, Mrs McRobbie?'

'Oh, yes; you see, we have all the folk up in Scotland, and then Carter has many friends in England that he made at school and college. He was at an old school called Shrewsbury, you know, in Shropshire. His father picked out the very oldest he could find so as the boy could learn *tradition*. He was always saying, bless his heart, that tradition was the strongest force in the world and if you learnt it young and learnt the best of it, you'd be bound to come out right in the end.'

'Did he, really?' commented Mrs Morley, pleasantly, not in the least understanding what 'tradition' meant. 'And is the teaching good there?'

'Well, I'm afraid Carter was never much hand at lessons, but then his father didn't set so much store by learning and manners as the other. But you must excuse me! Here are some Vancouver people just arrived.'

The new arrivals from the mainland brought with them such a spicy bit of news that they were very soon the centre of interest, and presently nothing else was talked about at Mrs McRobbie's reception but the horrible murder that had just taken place in Vancouver.

It seemed that a China boy had turned upon his mistress when alone in the house with her and slain her with a chair, after which he had further augmented his crime by the peculiarly revolting way in which he had disposed of his victim's body. The distracted husband had searched in vain for his wife until he came at last on a carefully folded heap of clothes hidden away in the basement. Suspecting foul play, he had raked out the ashes and found jewelry and – bones!

All Vancouver was athrill with horror at the ghastly circumstances of the murder, and it was enhanced by the fact that the China boy had been in the service of Mrs Smith, his victim, for years, during which time she had shown him especial kindness in teaching him herself and allowing him to attend a night school.

'Oh, Gordon!' cried Rose Morley, when describing the news to her husband later, 'what a mercy you never let me have a China boy! Why, it might just as easy have been me as Mrs Smith. Only three weeks ago I met her at a tea, and now to think of her all chopped up and put in the furnace by that yellow devil? Gracious heavens! I'll never be able to bring myself to go into another home with one in as long as I live!'

'Oh, come now, Rose, that's silly,' said her husband. 'There are just as black crimes committed every day by white people. You can't make out that all Chinks are devils just because one of them's turned out bad. Look at Crippen; he did the same thing, and you don't avoid all white folk because of him. As for Chinks, why, you can't get away from them! I'll bet half the cooks here are Chinks, just as all the call-boys are Japs!'

'I'll find out before I eat another meal,' exclaimed Rose, 'and if they are, I'll leave the hotel and go to another!'

It was, however, only too true. There were a good many China boys in the Empress kitchens, and Rose Morley kept her word and put herself to the trouble of moving to another and humbler hostelry, although it nearly broke her heart to leave the prestige of the magnificent Empress.

The repulsion that came over Mrs Morley attacked a good many others in the same way. The incident caused a wave of feeling against Orientals all over the country. Private householders who had employed China boys for years dismissed them on the spot right and left. Hotels were obliged to employ white help and swear they had no other or lose their entire clientele. Restaurants were obliged to placard their doors and windows with notices setting forth the fact that no other but white help was employed therein.

Hundreds of Chinamen were thrown suddenly out of work, and the trial of the murderer was awaited with a tremendous interest and suspense in Vancouver, by yellow and white alike.

Chapter 11

In which one Chinaman escapes justice and another gets a government job

THE TRIAL OF Sam Wong for the murder of his mistress was a *cause célèbre* that occupied many days. The counsel for the defence was that famous barrister, Craddock Low, who invariably undertook all the Chinese criminal cases, and every day the court was packed to overflowing with whites and Chinese.

The evidence showing the causes that led up to the altercation between Sam and Mrs Smith was disjointed and uncertain, as it was unwitnessed, but there was talk of a missing piece of jewelry, of a threat on the part of the woman, of Sam picking up a chair to defend himself, all of which was highly improbable and as little likely to be believed as Sam's assertion that Mrs Smith had wilfully crashed her own skull in against the chair while it was in his hand.

But a fresh thrill of horro rand down the spines of the listeners at the placid and almost amiable way in which Sam recounted his actions in disposing of the body.

'Me tly pushee Missee in furnace door – too big, no can do' – he shook his head with a smile; 'bym-bye me pullee off allee dless, foldee up, put him 'way tidy, no can see. Me go catchee good sharp knife, make him velly sharp' – here he suited the action to the word while his audience listened with morbid fascination – 'choppee Missee up in velly li'l bits all same cully, pushee li'l bits in furnace, can do velly good; savvee?'

Some few more observant than the others remarked that Craddock Low was a little nervous, even through his brilliant and masterly speech in defence of the crime, although none but the Chinese present noticed how often his eyes strayed across to that section of the court in which they were sitting and met the narrow eyes of one Chung Lee, inscrutable and inexorable, fixed upon him much as a cat watches the mouse that is feebly and ineffectually struggling in his paws.

The sentence pronounced by the judge raised a storm of protest in the town, but nothing could be done. Such had been the excellence of the defence that a verdict of 'manslaughter in justifiable self-defence' was brought in against the prisoner. Sam Wong got off with a short six years; the murdered woman's husband left the country with a vow of revenge against such gross injustice on his lips; Craddock Low congratulated himself and breathed freely again, and Chung Lee went his way smiling to himself a wise and subtle smile of satisfaction.

In nine days the horror of it all died down, in a few short weeks it was forgotten, and within two or three months Chinamen were as much in demand as ever, both in private houses and in public hotels and restaurants.

In the excitement of the elections and the subsequent busy time of the session, the little matter arranged between Craddock Low, Gordon Morley and Carter McRobbie during a lunch on board the latter's yacht, regarding the importation of an odd couple of hundred Chinese, had been put on one side.

But on a certain evening, after dinner, Craddock Low and Gordon Morley found themselves talking this matter over in a far corner of the palm room in the Empress Hotel in Victoria. The band played soft music and a rustling fountain sprayed silver showers close by them. At the various little tables sat couples or parties laughing and talking over coffee, iced drinks, liqueurs or cocktails.

Outside in the great saloon people passed to and fro on their way to the dining-room or sat about watching each other and listening to the music. There were rich tourists on a leisurely tour round the world, patrician Britishers who walked about as if there were nobody else in the room but themselves, business men from the mainland who used the hotel merely as a meeting-place, financiers from across the border with their wives and daughters, the latter very self-conscious in dresses obviously bought for the trip and trying in vain to look at home in them; little settlers from up country on a holiday, dressed in clothes that might have figured in a fifteen-year-old *Punch*, but thoroughly enjoying the sights of a city after years of the backwoods.

'About these head taxes, Craddock,' the MP was saying, 'supposing we got in just two hundred through this old guy you know of, well, with the head tax at $500 each, that comes to $100,000 — a bit stiff, you know, eh? Fifty thousand dollars wouldn't mean much, p'raps, to McRobbie, a rich man like him, but it would to me, and I tell you straight I don't feel like plunkin' down that much in a lump sum before a Chink, even knowin' it's a good investment!'

The lawyer leaned back and laughed a little at the other. He drained his cup of coffee and then, leaning forward with his elbows on the table, he said in a low tone, 'It's pretty evident *you* don't know as much about the Chinese immigration laws as an MP *should* know, Gordon! Haven't you heard of the merchants' clause that allows a Chinese trader to come in free if he can prove he's a merchant? Of course that means that he's got to spend a bit on bucksheesh to hush up the Paul Prys, but it can be done. And then there's another clause, "CI 9," that allows Chinks to go and visit their happy homes on t'other side and return within the year on payment of $1. Do you really believe, my innocent cherub, that all Chinamen who come into Canada pay a head tax?'

The MP gave a low whistle and allowed his heavy jaw to break into a slow smile.

'Gosh, you've got this thing pat, Crad.!'

'Sure! It's my business to get things pat! And lookee here, Gordon — his voice dropped and the two leaned still further over the table — 'we needn't worry friend McRobbie with all these details. It's kind o' born in on me that he's a boy with what they call a conscience somewheres, and he'd just hate to be found hoodwinking the Dominion Government. We'll let him pay up his lump sum in head taxes — he won't feel it, as you say — and we'll use some of it to oil the wheels so they won't creak, and the balance — well, I daresay you and I can find a use for the balance between us!'

The two men looked round them a little furtively, but there was no fear of eavesdropping here. At that very moment they were being pointed out as 'the brilliant MP who had risen on his own merits, probably discussing affairs of state with the most successful barrister in Briitish Columbia.'

'What's the name of this yellow guy you know of who's going to see this matter through for us?' asked Morley, rolling himself a cigarette.

'Young Lung Kow. He's as cunning as a coyote and as safe as a church. I made an appointment with him to see us tonight, and it's about time we were going now. Shall we git?'

The two went out of the hotel and down through the gardens out onto the causeway facing the little inner harbor, where the thousand eyes of night twinkled at the mastheads of boats, great and small. They turned up Government Street and followed it until they came to that end of it known as Chinatown.

The lawyer stopped at last before the shuttered windows of a Chinese curio shop. A dim light shone out through the chinks of the shutters. At the lawyer's tap the door was slowly and cautiously opened and the two visitors passed in.

A Chinaman stood before them bowing to the ground, a man of some mysterious age in the forties, wearing large spectacles that successfully concealed any hint of expression – if any ever showed in those opaque Oriental eyes.

But the eyes of Young Lung Kow never changed to suit the automatic grin that he deemed it advisable for his face to register periodically. It was little Bobbie Morley who said one day when he went with his father to the immigration office, 'Daddy, why is that Chink always smiling while his eyes are frowning?'

On his head was a little black silk cap from underneath which his pigtail reached down below his knees. He was clad in a priceless mandarin coat of saxe-blue silk embroidered with red and gold and purple dragons and bound in black, pantaloons to match and soft silk slippers. Beside the two westerners Young Lung Kow stood in sharp contrast as the symbol of the age-old civilization of the East.

He was of a suave politeness, polished and easy, that left his two bluff western visitors a little embarassed, more especially as he spoke their own tongue rather better than they did themselves. He took them thro' the shop, where was kept only merchandise to attract the common herd, into a set of inner chambers so furnished that the newcomers felt they must have been transported to the Orient. The atmosphere was heavy with the scent of joss-stick and ancient eastern odours that had almost the effect of deadening the brain. He insisted on showing them some Cloisonne ware that he had just imported, worth a mint of money, some unique brasses from a temple in the Pe-Ling Mountains, jade treasures from Canton, Satsuma vases that no one could possibly afford to buy.

Suddenly Young Lung stopped talking and bade his visitors be seated at a great table of black teak polished so they saw their faces in it as in a glass. The sides of it were carved and the legs of it were grinning dragons with forked tongues. They sat on chairs to match and the Chinaman, instead of seating himself in the ordinary way, stood for half a second facing his chair and in the twinkling of an eye he had seated himself, turned the right way round with his legs tucked beneath him, all in one movement, strangely agile.

He clapped his hands, and a silent-footed servant glided in with cups of tea on a tray, milkless, sugarless and without handles. By that time Craddock Low and Gordon Morley had almost forgotten what they had come for, they felt a little somnolent and heavy.

An hour afterwards they found themselves walking down Government Street again, having left behind them a signed and witnessed promise that bound Gordon Morley to use his powers as MP to appoint Young Lung Kow to the position of Assistant Controller of Customs at the Port of Victoria. In this position it would fall to him to register the names of all Chinese entering Canada, and in return for this he undertook to import two hundred of his fellow-countrymen free of head-tax for the benefit of Gordon Morley.

The MP was as good as his word in this matter and the appointment of Young Lung was ratified shortly afterwards.

Thus and so it was done. The foundations for the sale of British Columbia into the hands of the Orientals were laid – by Politicians whose sole aim was self-glorification, power, money; little souls with brains top-heavy with cunning, using their country and their fellows as stepping-stones to notoriety and a big bank account; by Capitalists who exploited the riches of their country and the necessities of the people in order that they themselves might profit, and live in ease and luxury, who denying all the responsibilities of wealth and power lived merely by the rule of Devil-take-the-hindmost; by every citizen who shut his eyes rather than see what he didn't wish to see, who, like the ostrich buried his head in the sand rather than face unpleasant truths and take a stand against them.

Part 2

The present (ten years after)

Chapter 12

In which we hear of a wedding and a death

MUCH WATER HAS PASSED under many bridges since the happening of the events recorded in our last chapter and men and things have changed since then in British Columbia as elsewhere.

The Great War and the see-saw of circumstance had reversed the fortunes of many. Those that had been poor had become rich and those that had been employers of labour were now working for their daily bread. The greater part of the city of Victoria was now in the hands of the Chinese together with some of the best and biggest houses in the residential quarters, both here and in Vancouver.

Many a returned soldier plodding wearily along in search of a job felt his gorge rise at the sight of John Chinaman whizzing past him in a luxurious, high-powered car with his wife and family. Gone were pigtails and gone were the blue-clad celestials who, like Chung Lee of old, trotted through the cities with vegetable or laundry baskets swinging from their shoulder-yokes.

Their places were taken by up-to-date motor-cars painted with Chinese characters in gold lettering and filled with a business too large to be stuffed into baskets. No one ever saw now, in Chinatown or elsewhere, an Oriental dressed in anything but European clothes. The thriving Chinese silk and curio store that had given Lizzie Laidlaw cause to remark one summer afternoon ten years ago was now a flourishing concern wherein stood white girls at the receipt of custom behind the counter.

It had become one of many such all the way up Granville Street and the towns were swamped with Oriental stores trading in European merchandise and beating the white man at his own game.

Some of China's four hundred and forty-seven millions had begun to overflow, crushed out of their own country by famine, poverty, overcrowding, and had found their foothold good in a land across the seas where there were vast, unpeopled spaces and only nine millions of people.

Old Robert Laidlaw of Lulu Island was dead, and so also was Mrs McRobbie, full of years and glad to go. Carter McRobbie was away up in the Stikine country hunting big-horn when a newspaper reached him telling of Laidlaw's death.

He packed his grips and trekked out that evening, travelling day and night until he reached the Coast, but even so it was a month before he could get down to Vancouver. He found the hired man busy at the milking and as there was no one about he walked straight on and into the house without announcing himself.

Lizzie was washing dishes in the back kitchen when he called to her from the doorway. Turning at the sound of his voice he saw the long pent-up love of years glowing in her eyes, and smiled. She went to him quickly.

They were married the week after, very quietly and having left the farm in charge of a friend, they went South to Honolulu on the *Pride o' My Heart* to spend a glorified honeymoon.

The marriage caused enormous stir in social circles. The wealthy McRobbie had long been an enviable *parti* for the debutantes of two generations although as he was now something near fifty, the mothers had almost begun to give up hope. To think that he had been snatched, as they put it, from under very noses by some obsolete, middle-aged farm woman of whom no one had ever heard made them all furiously prejudiced against the new Mrs McRobbie.

Not the least so was Mrs Gordon Morley. Her husband's party had been out and in and out and in again since last we told of it. His career had more than fulfilled its promise and this time he was now Premier of BC. Mrs Morley was perfectly happy in that she reigned supreme in her political kingdom.

Her ideals had been attained, and her life was full, so she said, of charitable and social duties. She was president of half a dozen public organizations and the corner-stone of another half-dozen societies. The fact that her only son had been killed in the Great War in no way embittered the whole taste of life for her as it had done for her husband. She took it rationally and philosophically, but then she had ever loved herself and her pleasures rather than her boy.

For Morley, his son's death had turned the sweets of life to dust and ashes in his mouth. The telegram announcing it had arrived a few hours before the news of his election to the premiership; for the mother the excitement and importance of the later news took away much of the sadness of the former, in a sense even partly compensated for the blow Fate had dealt her. It gave her something else to think about and the thinking greatly helped to salve the pain in her heart.

But for the father it seemed that the first bitter news took away the reason for his life, that he had lived and striven for nothing now that the boy was gone. He received the other news with a sick indifference almost akin to disgust at the emptiness of everything in life now that he had climbed to the very top of the ladder and could see the world for what it was worth.

It escaped his wife's notice that the lines about his mouth had become bitter and cynical, and his eyes had taken on the jaded look one sees in the eyes of men who have lived — and lived in vain. His step grew heavy and lost its spring, his shoulders drooped and if he had been hard before, he now became as cast iron in his merciless trampling of men weaker than himself.

There was a day when one Douglas Ross called on the Premier as he sat in his office with his secretaries. Now Ross had been at school with Bobbie Morley, and had met him again in Flanders where they had fought side by side; it was he who had carried Bobbie out of the firing line when he had been shot and his was the arm on which Bobbie had died.

Having returned from the wars sans health, sans money and sans job, Ross had kept hope in sight for some time by earning a bare existence in divers ways, but an erratic memory due to shellshock and failing physical health from much the same causes rather handicapped him in the competition and he fell behind — and out, so that the day came when he even lost sight of hope.

Times were bad for returned soldiers. One saw them everywhere prowling round in search of jobs. People began to connect them with such terms as vagrants, won't-workers and wasters. Employers looked the other way very often when they saw a man with a badge come forward in reply to an advertisement.

It had been in Douglas Ross's mind when he came to Victoria to go to Premier Morley, tell him all he knew of his son's death and last minutes and at the same time — much as he hated to do it — ask him for a helping hand to some solid work. He put it off on account of rumours he heard concerning the manner of man that the Premier was, but there came a time when he took his last hope desperately in both hands and walked to the Parliament Buildings to see the man that sat supreme therein.

'And what can we do for you, Mr Ross?' the Premier asked, looking up from his desk impatiently at the other man standing before
him. And Ross's hope shrivelled suddenly at the harsh, ice-cold
tones; the remnant of courage that months of disappointment, ill-
health and poor living had left in him died out of his heart at the sight
of that sullen, bitter face with never a gleam of pity in the eyes. And
yet he saw again in this face before him faint traces of likeness to
that blood-stained, pain-drawn, young face that had lain on his arm
one long-past day.

'I was in Flanders – ' he began hesitatingly.

'Yes, yes, I gather that much from your button, very creditable
indeed! And what are you doing now, may I ask?'

The Premier's glance had already gone back to the papers before
him. His own boy had not come back, so the sight of soldiers that
had returned rather irritated him than otherwise.

'Nothing,' Ross replied, speaking with that faltering uncertainty
that, to the successful, is the hall-mark of failure, 'that is – I was
hoping that perhaps you might be able to – ' He broke off lamely.
The great man had turned round to speak of something entirely
different to one of his secretaries. Then he looked up at Ross again.

'Look here, Mr Ross, we are very busy here this afternoon, as you
can see. You must pardon me, I have very little time to spare for
anything that is not actually pressing. *Good day!*'

Douglas Ross turned and went out of the room, shutting himself
carefully and quietly outside the door. He stumbled downstairs
again, dazed with despair, and walked and walked for hours till he
dropped in a heap at the end of a street. He was picked up by some
of the Salvation Army who cared for him in such wise that for sheer
animal gratitude that was piteous in its desire to please, he joined
their band for as long as he was able, but very soon he went West to
join Bobbie Morley who, one hopes, gave him the welcome his father
had refused.

And so Gordon Morley turned down yet another chance of
redemption offered him by Fate and unwittingly put away from him
the very salve that might have soothed the grizzling ache in his
empty heart. But that was the manner of man he was.

Meanwhile Mrs Morley went her gilded way with complacent
satisfaction. There were no houses now to which she had not the
right of entry through her position; she was also the wife of a very

wealthy man, so she basked in the sun and patronized everybody, envying no one, except perhaps the wife of the Lieutenant-Governor.

Strange to say she had never become intimate as she would have liked at the house of McRobbie and after the old lady died the house had seldom been used. The news of Carter McRobbie's marriage to Lizzie Laidlaw came on her, therefore, with the effect of a bombshell. To think that a middle-aged nobody of a farm girl who she, Rose Morley, had long since reckoned as one of her cast-offs, should step straight into the shoes of the one woman she had kow-towed to in vain! It thoroughly upset her when she had to believe it.

Chapter 13

Which tells of an elopement

THERE WAS A HOME in Vancouver in which was weeping, wailing and gnashing of teeth. A man and his wife sat either side of a table. The man in utter despondency, his head drooped on his breast and staring with unseeing eyes at the floor, his arms hanging helplessly at his sides, the woman openly sobbing into her handkerchief. The man we have met before. He was Harry Hart, then plain-clothes man, now sheriff of a municipality.

Their daughter Eileen had made a run-away marriage and they had only heard of it that morning. Now, plenty of daughters elope and reduce their parents to tears by so doing, return after a discreet interval, are forgiven and live happily ever after. But there was an element of tragedy, of such hopeless despair in the attitude of these parents that even knowing nothing of the facts one would have realised there was something unusually sad about this particular elopement. And there was. Pretty Eileen Hart, the pride of her mother, the apple of her father's eye, and only eighteen years old, had run away and married – a Chinaman. The horror of it turned them sick. She had been better dead. Eileen, with her beauty, her daintiness, her originality – they had always been specially proud of this and her daring – was now Mrs Wong Fu!

Mrs Hart had gone off into a dead faint when the letter came from Seattle whither Eileen had gone, supposedly to stay with a friend. The letter told how Wong Fu was an old schoolfellow, how, even in those days, he had always helped Eileen with her sums and thus won her childish affection and admiration. It told how she had met him periodically since she had left school, how he had been to college and then to China and back and what a good position he had – and how rich!

On the fifteenth reading of the letter, the mother-heart decided there was too much talk of the pearls and the Overland car he had given her, of the grand house they were going to buy on their return to Victoria, of the $5,000 a year he was to settle on her – and too little mention of her happiness.

'I just think it's *downright wicked*,' said the letter, 'for folks to look down on Chinamen the way they do! They're *just* the same as us and a deal better some of them! You just see how the girls will envy me when they see me riding round in my dandy car and queening it over everyone! Wong is *as good as a Prince* in his own country, *very* high up among the grandees, he says!'

But nothing could lighten the misery and the shame of the parents. They waited wretchedly for her next letter. But when it did come it was even more of a shock than the first one. On a day when their anxiety was stretched to breaking point came a crumpled bit of torn paper in a very dirty creased envelope unstamped and addressed to Mr Hart.

On the paper inside was scribbled in pencil the words: '*Daddy, come and fetch me away quick, or I shall die. Wong has four other wives and they are beastly to me. They watch me every minute so I can't run away, and I'm never alone. I think I'm in Victoria, but not sure, and I don't know the street or the number, as I'm never allowed to go out. Please come as quick as you can, Daddy dear!*'

The neighbours were called in to Mrs Hart, who went into raving hysterics, while Hart dashed off to Victoria by the first boat. The only clue he had to work upon was the Victoria post-mark on the letter. The poor man was half demented with misery when he rushed into the Premier's office and demanded a private interview at once.

Morley's suggestion was a posse of special police to make a house to house search all through Chinatown systematically. Hart suggested that Morley should exert all his private influence with every Chinaman he personally knew – and none knew better than Hart how large this circle was – to find out the exact whereabouts of Wong Fu.

As a matter of fact both suggestions were carried out, to a certain degree. The police drew a blank in Chinatown and went on, vainly endeavoring to locate every house outside it in other parts of the town and suburbs that belonged to a Chinaman. But no one had even heard of Wong Fu.

On the other hand, every prominent Chinaman was interviewed, including even the great Young Lung Kow himself. Suave and deferential as ever, he waved his hands deprecatingly at a quest which he likened to 'seeking the daughter of a silkworm in Fu-Chow.' Did the gracious gentlemen know the Tong of Wong Fu, he asked. Or from what Province in China he came? It were well, he said, with a little smile, to find out first whether such a man existed before looking for him.

Harry Hart grew desperate. He even threatened the Premier with the exposal of certain incidents from the past whereof he knew, if the Province was not immediately turned upside down and the missing daughter located. Morley shrugged his shoulders. He was not afraid now of blackmail, there were too many easy ways of getting rid of Hart, should he prove troublesome. He suggested a conference with the lawyer who was an expert in Chinese cases and an amalgamation with the police in Seattle and the best detectives, in the search.

'It's all the result of this *damned system of co-education,*' said Hart, 'and co-education along with the spawn of those yellow dogs, too! The Government schools are crowded out with Japs and Chinks. I know one school in Vancouver where there are *more Japs than white children!* Why the hell should *we* pay to have them educated and then suffer for it like this into the bargain, eh?'

'Well,' said Morley, 'they pay the taxes we do, why shouldn't they be entitled to the same privileges? You can't prevent it! We can't take their taxes and keep 'em out of the schools!'

'*It's the like of you* that have swamped the country with them doggone Chinks, Gordon Morley!' Hart cried desperately, all caution flung to the winds long since. 'They were bad enough when they were kept under as labour, but now they're getting education along with our own, they're a million times worse! They're uppish now, you even see that in the yellow brats coming out of school; they're cleverer than us and they know it and *you and I know it too!* Specially the Japs, you'll see them at the top 'o the class and the white kids at the bottom every time! There's a school in Vancouver were there's 324 Jap and Chink children to 275 whites, a precious fat chance *they* got to keep their end up! *Mighty good for both,* ain't it?' He rested his hands on the table and leant over with his face close to Morley's as he spoke the last words with a sneer.

Gordon Morley laughed shortly.

'Pooh! man, you're making too much of it. You'll feel different when you've got your girl back, as you will before long. Girls don't get lost in BC these days!'

'Oh! don't they? *You* know mighty well they do, too! If 'twas your girl you wouldn't be so almighty sure, either! You know as well as me what the Chinks do to white girls they get into Chinatown – *never see the light o' day again*, most o' 'em! *You* never made a law preventin' Chinks from havin' more'n one wife while they're livin' in our country, did you? *You* know they can all have as many's they want and what's more 90 per cent o' their women are not wives at all, they're *prostitutes!* An its the brats o' such as are allowed to go to school and grow up alongside our own and spill their morals over ours like a stinkin' disease!'

'Oh, Gosh! Their morals are no worse than the white man's. Don't pretend you're a saint, Harry!'

'*You speak for yourself*, Gordon Morley,' Hart's voice rose with his temper. 'I'd be sorry for the Chink whose morals are as rotten as yours, I would so! But even *you* never had the gall to keep your mistresses out in the open under the protection of the law like you allow the Chinks to do – like this godamned Wong Fu that's got my girl –.' The man's voice broke in a sob that shook him.

While he had been speaking Morley's fighting jaw thrust forward and his brows came down over his eyes in a scowl.

'You got some nerve, Harry, haven't you, to speak words like that to *me*, even if I wasn't the Premier of BC!' His voice was very soft and low. 'Seems to me you better get out of here while the getting's good, see!' and he pointed to the door.

Hart lifted up his fist and moved it slowly backwards and forwards at the other.

'*May the Lord break you and crush you and treat you as you deserve, Gordon Morley!* It's you as have sold this land bit by bit into the hands of the Chinks to fill your own pocket and build a gilt pedestal for yourself to stand on like the Judas Iscariot you are! *Curse you and all filthy skunks like you!*'

Then he went and the Premier sat down again with his chin on his hand, gazing at the shut door without moving for several minutes.

Hart went back to Vancouver by the night boat and soon after was at Craddock Low's house demanding an immediate interview. It was said that Low, erstwhile the most brilliant barrister in BC, had made so much money that he only kept on his practice as a hobby, which he took up now and again when he felt so inclined.

Be that as it may, he was not often seen in the courts and there were some funny rumours about as to midnight orgies in his house and queer guests therein who were very certainly not of his own complexion.

Hart had not set eyes on him for many months and when the lawyer came into the room the other was struck with the change in his appearance. Low's face was emaciated and sallow as a man looks when he lives on a surfeit of dissipation. His eyes looked black because the pupils were so dilated as to leave no room for the iris, and there was a strange glaze over them that gave him the look of a sleep-walker.

There was something about his shoulders, too, that struck Hart as curious, though his mind was so full of his trouble at the time that he paid little attention to it. It was not that the lawyer stooped, but his shoulders were raised in a curious way, giving the effect that his neck was shorter behind than it was in front.

Hart stated his case as briefly as possible and asked advice as to the best course to follow.

To his horror, instead of giving the shocked sympathy he expected, the lawyer leered, actually leered. A knowing smile came over his face and he winked at Hart as he said, 'Cute old Wong, pretty little white girl! Bet he's having a good time now, eh, Harry!'

Hart exploded. He went close up to the other, standing stiff with his fists clenched.

'You just such another dirty dog as Gordon Morley, eh!' But, strange to say, Craddock Low did not even then change his attitude. He went on leering, and, as if enjoying a huge joke, muttered again:

'*They* know how to get 'em! Pretty little Eileen, nice and young and fresh! *They* know how —' A stunning blow under the chin stopped him and Hart rushed out of the house, leaving Craddock Low crumpled up on the floor like a heap of dirty clothes.

The police of Vancouver, Victoria and Seattle searched with sympathetic and untiring energy every nook and cranny of every Chinese house they knew of in the three towns till the days stretched into weeks, and the weeks into months, but in vain. Eileen Hart was never heard of again, and Harry Hart was warned to betake himself and his wife outside Canada in the shortest possible time — or forever to hold his peace.

Chapter 14

Showing the perspicacity of Peter McReady

ON A SUNNY SPRING afternoon an old river stern-wheeler was puffing her busy way up the Fraser River. It was a little early in the year for those who went up that way on a pleasure trip, so all aboard were on divers business bent.

Two men leant over the taffrail for'ard, smoking and exchanging a remark now and then. One of them was our old friend J.B. Harding of the Fisheries Board, whom we met before up North when he was going his rounds as Inspector. Since then he had been to the war and come back with signal distinction for services rendered in connection with secret service work.

He was one of the lucky few who had been able to get back to his old job when all the militarism was over and we see him now on his way up the river to examine the waters of the Yale Canon, which had been shamefully blockaded a year or so ago with disastrous results by those with more nets than wits, who called themselves fishermen.

His companion was an old man whom we have also met before. He was that same Peter McReady who had kept the store at Bella Bella and kept it with such purpose that, with the advance of years, he found himself able to retire with dignity and comparative affluence.

It was not quite by chance that they found themselves together on board; they had run up against each other two or three days before in the lobby of an hotel in Vancouver and Harding had mentioned the trip he was about to take.

'The Yale Canyon?' McReady had said, 'Well now, seeing it's all of twenty-seven years since I set eyes on it, I've a notion to come along with you. Look out for me and see if I don't!'

And he was as good as his word. Just now, as the steamer was nearing the railway bridge across the river at Mission, he was recalling the day when there were no bridges at all across the Fraser and the houses on its banks as 'far apart as strawberries in January.'

'Them were the good days all the same,' he said, 'when a chap was always worth his good day's work and a white man was chosen before any other colour! You never heard tell *then* of a yellow man owning land. No sir, the yellow and the brown were kept in their place then and kept to themselves, believe me!'

'They tell me that 50 per cent of the fruit round here is produced by Japs,' commented Harding, 'and this district on the north side of the valley is the very heart of the best small fruit country in the Province. We're a bright lot, aren't we, Pete?'

'Sure we are, and that's true, too about the fruit. A chap I know as lives at Hatzic was telling me that there were only two or three Japs who owned land round there ten years ago, and now there are between forty and fifty! One hundred and fifty on 'em 'round Mission — *landowners*, look you — and as thick as thieves in Maple Ridge District and Haney and Hammond and way up beyond to Nicomen! Funny, ain't it, how sleepy we'se all are?'

'Yes, but it won't look funny in another few years if we don't wake up! The Japs as landowners are rather worse than the Chinese, because the Chinks at any rate do centralize and stick to their own quarters, but the Japs buy here and there and everywhere, and then the white men they settle next have to turn out. You just can't live next door to a Jap family — not for long!'

Old McReady chuckled and refilled his pipe from his little bag of Old Chum.

'Now lookee here, John Harding,' he said, 'you know just 'bout enough of the Japs to know they haven't got to where they are in the world today — one of the three almighty grandest powers and all that done in fifty years — by using any old slipshod methods and buying land here, there and everywhere without no plan behind it!'

'You're right there Pete, but what do *you* know about it, in this particular land business, I mean?'

'Why, sposin' they wants to get hold of a certain road, one Jap will buy a plot, cleared or uncleared, good or bad, at one end of it, another buys at t'other end. There's never a white man as won't be bought out for a price. Then the neighbours o' these Japs moves out, t'aint, as you say, nice and pleasant livin' next door to a Jap. Well, other Japs moves in where the whites have moved out an' so on gradually, till they close in nearer an' then the white man left in the middle all alone among a colony o' Japs has to move out in self-defence, and next thing you know the Japs ha' got *that* road!'

Harding shook his head seriously.

'Is that the way they're working it in this district?' he asked.

'Sure thing! I told you I got a pal in the fruit business at Hatzic.'

The local freight being loaded and unloaded, the little boat moved away from the wharf at Mission and proceeded on her way up river.

The afternoon sun shone down on white-walled bungalows with their red roofs, standing in the midst of sloping fields of raspberries or logans in rows straight as darts, each row with its little wooden cross at the end of it upon which the wires were tied. Acres and acres of every imaginable variety of berry fruit sloping far up the mountain side, backed by the dark green forest and still further beyond by glistening snow peaks.

Away to the right as far as the eye could see stretched the flat fertile farm lands of the valley, prosperous and peaceful.

'See that big white house up there with the queer flat roof?' asked McReady, pointing up at a certain house far up on top of a hill. 'Well, that's the self-same identical house we came up to one dark night twenty-seven years ago, me an' a pal, one time we was hikin' down to the Coast. An' the folks as lived there then – they're dead an' gone now – they jest made us as welcome as if they was settin' there expectin' us to come! Took us in an' cooked a special lunch for us an' all, they did! We two was jest 'bout all in that night, I guess, too sleepy to wonder where we was, but I rec'lect now the way we woke up in the morning and looked out o' the window to see that view across there.'

He waved his hand towards the other bank.

'Yes, the view from there must be fine,' said Harding. 'I expect you can see a long way from up there.'

'Fine, man! It *just takes your breath away!* You can see way over miles upon miles of country – it was all bush or beaver meadow and swamp them days – right across south as far as the border down to Blaine. Look that way to the mountains this side o' Sumas Lake and you see Mount Cheam behind the Chilliwack Valley. And the river winding below like a big silver ribbon.'

'I must go up there one day and see it. And I suppose you can see even further from up there?' Harding pointed to the top of a bluff several hundred feet higher than the white-walled house. 'Look, up there where you can see those men working!' And sure enough, far up on the top of the mountain were to be seen the little figures of men working, outlined against the sky.

'Gee, what a strategical position, eh?' Harding chuckled. His mind was still full of that habit of thinking engendered by war.

They still leant over the taffrail, looking up. Then McReady suddenly leant forward and looked a little harder and said, *'Gosh!'* in a heavy undertone.

'Look, man!' he whispered to Harding, clutching hold of his arm. 'look again and see if you don't notice anything about those men working up there, and *remember what you said!'*

Harding made a telescope of his hands and gazed anew. Presently he dropped them and turned to his companion. The two men stood looking at each other.

'Japs!' whispered one.

'Yes, *Japs!'* whispered the other. 'They're too squat for white men, besides, whites don't run about their work like that!'

'Didn't I say there weren't no indiscriminate methods in their buying? There's always a reason when a Jap begins to act!'

'There sure looks as if there was a pretty good reason here all right! There's the Mission bridge, *the only bridge across the Fraser after Westminster!* If it was their object to buy positions to give them command of the only parts of the river it was possible to cross, they've got them all right and that's a cinch. At least they've got it up there. I wonder now, if by any chance they've got the land *up there* on the lower side of the bridge. If they have, it's *not chance*, and I'll begin to believe in their object!'

'Go and ask the skipper,' suggested McReady. 'He'll tell you if anyone can.'

He was right, the skipper knew well enough and was nothing loth to give away his information.

'Who owns that land up there?' he made answer. 'Why, Japs, just doggone Japs, pushing theirselves in all up this valley they are, and pushing the white man out!'

'Funny to see them buy up there,' Harding remarked, 'you'd have thought a Jap knew enough to buy the best bottom land in the country!'

'No,' replied the skipper, 'it's funny, but they seem to like the high land best. You don't find them on the south side of the river at all. But they got all the high land between Vancouver and Nicomen right along the river!'

Harding went back to McReady and they talked it over.

'Clever,' Harding said, 'clever, you know! The Fraser River is just one of the very first objectives one would have in mind if one wanted to take BC! Why, it's not only one of the gateways in, but it's one of the principal veins of the country geographically! An army attacking BC from the south would have no chance whatever of crossing the river if the heights on the north shore were in possession of the other forces, it would be easy enough to burn both the bridges!'

'*Now* you know why the Japs haven't bought on the south shore!' remarked the old man grimly, 'and *now* you know why they got such a hold down at Steveston – in the name o' fishin' – that a white man dursn't show his face there at the mouth o' the river in the season, an' only on sufferance at any other time! Why, it's a regular Japanese colony down there!'

'We must look further into this business, Pete, strikes me there's more than coincidence in it, same as there was about the sampans!'

They went on up the river to the Yale Canyon and came back to Vancouver, where they arranged to carry out a few judicious enquiries in their own respective ways. Old Pete, who had friends right along the water-front and cronies in most of the dives and dens of Vancouver's underworld, was useful in gathering knowledge that Harding could not otherwise have obtained.

They met a few days afterwards, in the lobby of the C– hotel, where Harding usually stayed, and exchanged information. The results of their enquiries appeared to coincide and Harding's face grew graver and graver at the aspect of things.

They talked far on into the night and Harding's heart was heavy within him when at last he shook himself and went upstairs to bed. He was due to start off so early the following morning that he made certain preparations over night to save time. He remembered the film in his camera; he would unload it now and roll it up ready to leave with a druggist next morning on his way down to the station. In the morning it might be too late and he would be sure to forget it.

He looked round for a darker place in which to do this, for the room was small and the light very brilliant. There was a bolted door leading, he supposed, into a clothes closet or into the next room, anyway he unlocked it to see.

It was one of those tiny partitions between rooms, and the door of the next room directly faced him. There were two men next door talking and as the partition was so thin he could hear every word they were saying.

'Oh! well,' he thought to himself, as he stepped inside with his camera, 'they're not talking secrets anyway, and if they are they shouldn't talk so loud.'

The conversation was uninteresting, something about papering and refurnishing, one voice he recognised as that of Bateman, the manager of the hotel, and also owner, as everyone popularly believed.

'All rooms on this floor to be papered again, also new plumbing, see?' said one voice. 'All right, I'll see it's done.' Bateman's voice made answer.

'That's funny,' thought Harding vaguely to himself, busy with his camera, 'I always thought Bateman owned this place. Now it sounds as if he's taking orders from someone else!'

'Employ Clarke & Woolley,' went on the strange voice.

'Why not Johnson's? They did it last time, and did it well,' enquired Bateman.

'Do what I tell,' said the strange voice shortly and sharply, 'no reasons answered. Employ Clarke & Woolley without any fail!'

'Funny way of putting it,' thought Harding, his attention caught by the last sentence. 'Dashed if it isn't a foreigner that Bateman's taking his orders from!'

'All right, all right,' replied Bateman pacifically, 'no need to get ratty about it!'

'Give them cheque in your name, see, and I come and give you cash soon after. Now I go.'

Harding's curiosity got the better of him. He slung a towel over his arm as though going out for a bath and timed his door to open at the same time as the next door.

The man who came out of the other room was a Jap. He drew back for the fraction of a second when he saw Harding and then passed quickly across the passage with his head bent, and ran downstairs.

But that one sight of his face was sufficient to convince Harding that he had seen him somewhere before.

Chapter 15

Lizzie McRobbie shows an interest in 'Sockeye' and tries to buy vegetables

IT WAS ABOUT a week after this that Harding was strolling one evening through the lounge of the Hotel Vancouver, when someone touched his arm and spoke his name. He turned to see McRobbie, the wealthy salmon-canner.

'Hullo! Harding, it's a long time since we've met, isn't it? How's the fishing going? Glad to hear you got your old job back again when you returned from overseas! Come and let me introduce you to my wife!'

Harding found himself shaking hands with a fresh-complexioned woman with thoughtful eyes and a kind smile. McRobbie drew up another chair and they all sat down together. Harding made a mental comparison between this and that last time he had met the other up at River's Inlet. He had not forgotten McRobbie's peculiar treatment of him on that occasion.

'We're staying here a few days before we go up north; we're going up early this year. My wife has never seen River's Inlet, you know!'

'Is that so?' said Harding politely. 'She certainly has a treat before her.'

'I've been up very little myself lately, left it all to my manager during the war while I was back East helping in the recruiting office.'

'I expect you find, as I do, that conditions in the fishery business are very different nowadays to what they used to be? The output seems to have decreased pretty steadily in the last few years and sockeye's at a premium.'

McRobbie handed the other a cigarette and lit one himself before replying.

'Oh! well,' he said carelessly, throwing the match away, 'we let everything go in wartime. They've made a whole lot of new regulations now, so things will begin to brighten up again.'

'Yes,' said Harding, 'we managed to get the Premier to put that through last session anyway; about the best thing he's done since he's been in office!'

'He's not likely to be in office much longer if these rumors are correct!'

'What rumors?' asked Harding.

'That his private affairs are in a pretty groggy state. I've heard it on all sides lately, though I can't imagine how a successful old stager like Gordon Morley could let his finances go like that.'

'Poor man,' put in Mrs McRobbie, speaking for the first time, 'he's had a big lot of responsibility on him this long time, and an awful trouble in losing his boy. It's likely he speculated rashly and lost.'

She had a soft, slow voice with a trace of Scotch, both in accent and words, and when Lizzie McRobbie spoke people listened.

Her husband put out his hand and stroked her cheek with his finger.

'You'd find excuses for Old Nick himself, wouldn't you sweetheart?' he said, smiling.

Mrs McRobbie turned to Harding again.

'Did you mean,' she asked, 'that the stock of sockeye salmon is lower in proportion to what it used to be? That's strange, I wonder why!'

Harding looked at her with new attention. It was not often that women took an interest in fish.

'That puzzle can be solved in two words, Mrs McRobbie, *Jap fishermen!*'

'Ah! So that's it, is it? Just what father always said would happen, didn't he, Carter?

Her husband moved a little uncomfortably.

'Oh, if you two are fans on the Jap question, I'm off!'

Harding leant forward and tapped him on the knee.

'Look here, Mr McRobbie, your interests are bound up in the interests of this country, aren't they ? Very well, then, in the name of both you've got to listen to me for a few minutes, and when I'm through you'll be a 'fan on the Jap question,' too!'

And McRobbie had to listen.

'You know,' he said, when Harding had finished speaking, 'I think you ex-soldiers have your minds so full of war that you look upon everything with a militaristic eye! What on earth would the Japs want to invade Canada for? They know they can come and settle here quite peaceably if they like!'

'Yes, and they are coming – in numbers too big for us and too small for them! They've *got* to have somewhere to overflow into, some place to put their seventy-seven and a half millions that are increasing at the rate of four hundred thousand a year! This country suits them better than any other, why wouldn't they want it for themselves? It's only natural!'

'But man alive, you've forgotten there's an Anglo-Japanese treaty!'

'Treaty *nothing!* Did a treaty prevent the Great War? Not a bit of it!

For there is neither East nor West,
   Border, nor breed, nor birth,
When two strong men stand face to face,
   Tho' they come from the ends of the earth!'

'The only thing is,' said Mrs McRobbie who had been listening intently, 'that they wouldn't need to make a war of getting, they could *just walk in!* We've never a ship to defend our coasts and never a big gun on the land!'

Her husband laughed shortly.

'Oh, the Japs are much too polite to make war, they'd just walk in with a bow and say they'd come!'

'They're quite the most wonderful people in the world,' agreed Harding, 'and the most progressive! If they're wise – and I think they are far too clever to make the mistake the Germans did – they'll just keep on the way they are, and in a few years they'll have all the trade of the world in their hands and the whiphand of every country there is without any fighting at all!'

'Yes, we don't want any more war yet!'

'*The only way to prevent war*,' said Harding, 'is to be *prepared for it!* You don't see the Japs leaving anything to chance! Is it just by chance, d'you suppose, that all the highest land right along the Fraser River from Vancouver to Nicomen is in their hands? Is it just chance that their Government *lent them the money to buy it up?* Is it just chance that those loans have stopped lately because all the money in Japan is wanted to build a navy with?'

McRobbie looked frowning at the floor and made no answer. His wife and Harding went on talking.

Presently a Jap boy, one of the many employed at the Hotel, passed by dangling a bunch of keys. Harding happened to look up and saw him coming. He called the man up and asked him some trifling question.

McRobbie gave an exclamation as the man approached.

'Why, if it isn't my old friend, Hoshimura!' he cried.

But the Jap's stolid face didn't brighten, not even by the flicker of an eyelid did he betray any sign of recognition. He shook his head.

'Gen'leman make mistake. My name Omara!' And with a bow he went off.

'Well, I could have sworn that was my old Jap manager at the cannery, Hoshimura!' said McRobbie, non-plussed.

'It *was* Hoshimura,' said Harding, 'would it surprise you to know that he owns the C— Hotel?'

'*What?*' exclaimed McRobbie, sitting up and clutching the arms of his chair.

And 'How do you know that, Mr Harding?' his wife asked with no less interest.

'The fact forced itself upon my notice, Mrs McRobbie, I'm afraid it's perfectly true and just shows that the Jap, like the Chinese, have progressed a long way beyond "labor" in this country!'

'Hoshimura own a *hotel, right here in this city?*' expostulated McRobbie again. 'Why it's preposterous, though I suppose after all he was earning pretty good money up North and if he saved it all – well it's not impossible! But what the nuisance is he doing in this place as a *bell-boy?*'

'Oh, that's only a blind, it's easy work and he prefers to do something rather than nothing!'

McRobbie was more startled than he cared to admit. Somehow the bit of information had considerably altered his aspect of things; it put the whole question on a different footing, shook it up and turned it topsy-turvy. The very foundations of his former world seemed not so stable as they had been. He discussed the question now from a different angle.

When Harding rose to go, Mrs McRobbie bade him goodbye with obvious regret. She made him promise to visit them in Victoria.

'You love this country, Mr Harding?' she asked him.

'I ought to,' he replied, 'I fought for it and saw my pals die for it, and I should just hate to see it pass out of our hands!'

'As my father used to say, there are many who *talk* but few that *act!* I think you are one of the latter, Mr Harding, we mustn't lose sight of you. I have a notion the country has need of you still, and that is why you were spared, don't you think so, Carter?'

McRobbie, of course, agreed with her heartily, as he did with everything she said, and Harding went on his way warmed and cheered.

It so happened that Mrs McRobbie went out next morning to visit old friends who lived in a humble way in half a house down Burrard Street. She found her friend who was an invalid with her couch drawn up to the window trying to enjoy a two foot square patch of sunlight the short while it lasted in her room.

'Oh, Liz darling, you're a sight for sore eyes in this dingy place! Here am I trying my best to make believe I'm back on the farm but I'm afraid my imagination isn't as strong as it should be!'

Mrs McRobbie drew off her gloves and sat down beside her. 'Yes,' she said with a sigh, '*I* know what it is to give up your farm when you've lived on it all your life! Even though I'm as happy as a queen and can have everything I want, I have spells of awful home-sickness for the cows and the bees and my garden! Not all the grand houses in the world can make up for it, but there, Carter was never cut out for a farmer, bless his heart!'

'It's the garden we miss most,' the other woman agreed, 'specially when you've made it all out of the bush! I just pant for it at this time o' the year, I know how the gooseberries will be hanging heavy on the bushes, and the big scented lilies will be blooming, and you can run out of the ‑kitchen door whenever you want and pick a bunch o' mint or parsley and an early lettuce nice and crisp for tea! Here you have to buy everything all faded at the door, and it's all that nasty Chinese stuff, which I just *can't* fancy, seeing that I know what I do know!'

'D'you mean about the way they manure it?' asked Mrs Mc-Robbie. 'Yes, I've heard something of that too!'

Mrs Brown whispered something that made her screw up her face in disgust. 'But are you sure it's really true?' she asked.

'Certain, Donald's seen them do it! They go round Chinatown at night collecting it from door to door in barrels and take it out in carts to their gardens outside the city!'

'Heavens! I shall never eat another vegetable unless I make sure it's not grown by the Chinese!' exclaimed Mrs McRobbie.

'I've said the same, my dear, and as a result I've just had to cut myself off them altogether, for the landlady only buys them at the door, and no one but Chinamen come around. I can't get out myself to look round from store to store and Don hasn't the time!'

'But gracious, Dora, that's not good for you, vegetables are necessary for health! Now I'll tell you what I'll do. I'll go round to the stores this very morning and buy some for you at a place where they deal with a white gardener, and then you can deal with him always!'

But Mrs Brown shook her head and smiled.

'You're a dear, Liz, to offer, but I'm afraid you'll have your work cut out to find such a place!'

Lizzie McRobbie pooh-poohed the notion, and after some more talk, she set off on her quest. She well knew that there were no other travelling vendors of garden produce but the Chinese, so she went first of all to the big department stores.

The first two she visited told her openly that all their market-garden produce came from gardens owned by Chinamen who were under contract to supply them. The next store assured her that they bought everything from a white man; she made enquiries as to this and found that the said white man never went near his garden which was leased to and worked entirely by Chinese.

'But this is *awful*, Carter,' she said to her husband, 'to think there should be all this difficulty in buying vegetables raised by our own people! It's almost incredible! Why, I believe all the hotels deal with them exclusively too!'

She was right. At her request, McRobbie himself made enquiries and found that they bought either from a bigger store or from the wholesalers who in turn dealt with nobody but Chinese market gardeners.

After a week of fruitless search, Lizzie McRobbie gave it up. She was horrified and disgusted. She made arrangements for a weekly supply to be sent from her own farm to her friend in Burrard Street, and vowed that she herself would never stop in a hotel again until things were remedied.

'But Madam,' said the manager of the Hotel Vancouver, to whom she spoke on the subject, '*there is no remedy!* It doesn't pay a white man to grow vegetables, he can't compete with the Chinamen who are not only the best gardeners in the world, but live so much more cheaply that they don't ask so much profit! *They have a monopoly of the vegetable trade all over* BC, and of the potato market also; the white man has to feed his pigs on his potatoes when the Chinaman enters into competition! If you go up to the Okanagan Valley you'll see more white men working for Chinese masters on the land than ever owned vegetable patches for themselves!'

Chapter 16

In which there are many rumors and a few facts

FOR SOME LITTLE TIME there had been vague rumors abroad concerning the unsteadiness of the Premier's private financial affairs. Some said he had speculated too heavily in land and got tied up in the vagaries of real estate, others that he had financed some harebrained scheme and lost, but none knew the truth or were ever likely to find it out, Gordon Morley being the man he was.

Certainly the rumors never gained any ground from the aspect of the man or from any change in his mode of life. His eye was as hard and his jaw as set as ever, not a hint of the success or failure of his multitudinous private schemes had he ever been known to let drop to friend or foe. His wife still went her complacent way as luxuriously as before — no distress there, certainly no economy.

Still the rumor spread, but whether founded on fiction or fact no one knew. Then as a thunderbolt came a piece of news as startling as it was unexpected, shattering all these vague reports, confounding all the gossips.

On a certain day, people read in their newspapers the plain fact that the Hon. Gordon Morley, Premier of BC, had bought up the Pacific Sugar Refinery in Vancouver, the only one in BC.

Everybody, including Mrs Morley herself, was astounded beyond words by the news, they had had no idea that Morley was a millionaire, though most people had put him down as a bit of a dark horse. But the man himself went his way unperturbed.

Some few bolder souls ventured on a little chaff at the Union Club anent the secrecy of the deal, but it was like chaffing a stone wall. Gordon Morley was no joker and chaff failed to bring forth even a smile, indeed he was seldom seen to smile at all these days.

It was not very long after this that the Premier paid an unofficial visit to the Customs Houses and in particular to the office of the Assistant Controller of Customs who was, strangely enough, a Chinaman, still that same Young Lung Kow whom we met just before he was appointed to that post ten years ago.

Young Lung had never descended to the usage of European clothes. Although his pigtail was no more, he still showed his predilection for the flowing silks and manifold colours of his native land. Unctuous and urbane as ever, he had never been known to raise his voice, or to hurry or lose his customary calm or even to disagree with an expressed opinion. Yet he seemed invested with a mysterious power that gave him some sort of wizard hold on all the officials connected with the Port.

They would drop their voices when Young Lung Kow passed that way. The Chief Controller of Customs never dreamt of signing any document or report that had not been 'OK'd' by Young Lung; in short it became a habit with officials to consult with him upon every move of routine or otherwise, almost as though they were afraid of him or of incurring his displeasure.

When the Premier opened the door of his office, Young Lung rose and bowed to the ground, and went on bowing until Morley was seated. Then they spent much time looking over statistics together. There were some very interesting figures about the value of merchandise, imports and exports, and still more interesting about the number of Chinese immigrants into Canada during the year.

There were so many clauses of the Immigration Act that it was hardly surprising to find immigrants slipping in through by-clauses instead of the main clause. Many clauses but only two Gateways — Victoria and Vancouver, and Young Lung Kow was the keeper of one Gate.

For instance, against the few hundreds who had paid head-taxes in the legitimate way there were many thousands who had come in through Clause 9 which permitted Chinese resident in Canada to make a trip to their native land and return free of head-tax (on payment of $1.00) within the year, provided they were registered at the Port from which they sailed.

Young Lung Kow was the official who registered these pseudo-tourists; the other officials guessed that perhaps about two per cent of them had ever set eyes on Canada before, and that all the rest were newcomers evading the head-tax, but *they looked the other way*. Young Lung was a mighty unpleasant fellow to fall out with.

But this morning figures failed for once to attract the real attention of the Premier; he gave them but a cursory glance, he fidgeted as though he had something else on his mind, and presently he brushed the papers aside and spoke of this thing.

The Chinaman listened politely with narrowed black eyes that neither blinked nor left the other's face, and all the time he smiled. When the other had finished, he spoke, recalling certain matters of the past. He used logic, hard and irrefutable, cause and effect, action and result, leading up to his final words spoken in a harsh undertone.

'This thing *must be done*, Mr Morley!'

The Premier brought his fist down on the table.

'*I tell you it is impossible!*' he said gruffly, but there was that in his tone that suggested the snarl of a hunted animal caught in a trap.

'No,' the other contradicted smoothly, 'there is nothing impossible under the sun, least of all to Gordon Morley! Now is your chance. You are about to appoint a new Lieutenant-Governor. Appoint one who will do as *you* say, sign any bill *you* wish, be *your* tool!'

Morley sat silent, his elbow on the table, his hand shading his eyes. Then he rose and pushed back his chair noisily.

Young Lung stood before him, bowing to the ground. 'Come and see me at my house some night soon,' he was saying 'and tell to me what you have done!'

The Premier passed out of the room without a word.

That afternoon a few of the more influential members of the House met informally to discuss between themselves the nominations for a new Lieutenant-Governor. One of the names most favored was Carter McRobbie.

'He will give us least trouble,' said one.

'He has most to lose by resistance to our wishes,' said another.

'He is an amiable, pleasant sort of fellow who will make an excellent figure-head,' said another 'who will sign a bill with his eyes shut because it's too much trouble to read it through!'

'Yes,' said the Premier, 'I, too, am of the opinion that Carter McRobbie would suit us best!'

So the word went forth to Ottawa.

One evening shortly afterwards Gordon Morley called for his car and drove himself out to keep his appointment at Young Lung Kow's private house. On the way he stopped at an oil station for gasoline and as he waited he heard an altercation at the street corner between an Englishman, who in spite of prohibition was more than a little the worse for drink, and a Chinaman who was squirming to free himself from the grip on his coat collar.

'You nasty little wriggling toad of a yellow devil! *I'll teach you* to get in my way when I'm walking down the street!'

'Me go catchum pleecy-man,' whined the wretched Oriental. 'You lemme go now heap quick!'

'*You*, you couldn't go if you tried, you stinker! Whyn't you stay an' fight, eh! Fat lot o' good you blinkin' yellow dogs 'ud be in a war!'

And so saying he lifted his victim right off the ground, gave him another vicious shake and dropped him free.

The Chinaman turned to run, but before he fled he gave his final answer to his persecutor.

'*War heap good, killee plenty white man!*' he cried — and spat, and ran.

The tippler laughed and went meandering on his zig-zag way, but the man who listened waited beside his car, took that last remark differently. He drew in his breath sharply between clenched teeth and swore luridly, scowling after the disappearing figure of the Chinaman.

The house of Young Lung Kow was one of the most palatial on Highland Avenue, and was besides quite remarkable for its beauty of architecture among those many glaringly new seats of the mighty. A winding drive between flowering shrubs led up to the door, or rather, porticoed entrance, at one end of a tiled verandah which was intersected with arches and columns.

Morley was expected and the door was opened almost immediately in answer to his ring by a Chinaman dressed in white duck, the same man had bowed him into this house many a time before. The hall was barbaric in its Oriental splendour. A fountain tinkled in the middle of the room and the walls were hung with be-dragoned tapestries of gold and silver, red and purple and blue. Two or three heavy chairs of carved black teak were the only other furnishings.

The servant padded across the room in his straw shoes and held back a tapestry in the corner for Morley to pass through. In a room even more sombre and oppressively splendid than the hall, sat Young Lung Kow waiting for his guest.

The Canadian might have been a prince of the blood royal by the way he was greeted, the way refreshment and a choice of smokes was pressed effusively upon him. But he refused all these things and sat him down in a great carved chair with never a smile in return for his host's oily eloquence.

They talked, these two, far into the night. And ever it seemed that the Oriental was persuading the other to some course that was distasteful. After a while the argument took a more definite turn; the persuasions became threats, veiled in polite words it is true, still there was no doubt they were threats, while the attitude of the other changed from distaste to dislike, from dislike to scowling horror.

The Chinaman smiled always, but his eyes never changed. Morley's eyes glanced about the room as though he were looking for some loophole of escape from a trap. His jaw sagged a little, and presently he took out his handkerchief and mopped his forehead, though the room was cold.

'*Good God! You yellow devils!*' The words came huskily from him in gasps. 'I tell you I *can't* do it, *don't you understand that!*'

'There is no such word as "can't" for Gordon Morley, Premier of BC,' came in smooth tones falling like ice upon the heat of the other. 'You *can* and you *will* — or else, you know the alternative! Young Lung Kow keeps his word — if Gordon Morley doesn't!'

Morley rose and put a hand on the arm of his chair to steady himself. Then with a mighty effort he straightened himself and walked towards the door. Before he reached it, there was a servant bowing in front of it ready to show him out.

'The best of luck to yourself and our schemes, my friend!' said his host pleasantly behind him.

Morley turned on him then like a flash and shook his fist in the Oriental's face, his over-strained nerves almost at breaking point.

'*May you burn in hell, you and your devilish schemes, you spawn of worse than the devil!*' his voice was a husky scream and the knotted veins stood out on his brow.

On the instant, half a dozen Chinamen sprang from the floor it seemed, ready to protect their master in case of danger. Young Lung himself, however, showed no sign of fear. He laughed outright at his guest's parting shot.

'You also have served the devil, Gordon Morley, *against your own countrymen*, I at least have only used him to *help me serve my country!*'

Morley strode through the hall and out of the door into the clean night air where he stood a moment bare-headed and breathing deeply as though to rid his soul of the foul thing he had left behind.

He walked down the drive to his car a little uncertainly as tho' his knees trembled, and when he reached it he sat staring straight in front of him for a full five minutes. There was a rustle in the bushes near him, but though he heard and understood, he did not even turn his head. He was watched and he knew it, but he had been watched and followed for so many months now that he had become used to it.

At last he slipped in the clutch and drove like fury, back to the city.

Chapter 17

In which Rose's nose is put out of joint
and a man reaches the last stages

THE NEWS OF THE nomination of Carter Alastair McRobbie for the Lieutenant-Governorship was received in very different ways by that gentleman and his wife. He, himself was all for refusing the honour point-blank. He was not a man to whom flattery made any appeal, neither was he on the look-out for worldly honours, being completely happy in his present circumstances.

But his wife was of another way of thinking.

'It is your duty, my man,' she said to him, 'just as clear as the stars in the sky. Those who are rich like you must pay for it in responsibility some time or other. Seems to me that poor old BC wants a good man and strong at the helm just now, and the offer has come to you, Carter. If you turn it down you'll be shirking your bit the same as ever those laggards they called "conscientious objectors" did! Then they might take some weak, spineless fellow who played for himself instead of for the country.'

'And how d'you know I wouldn't prove 'weak and spineless' in responsibility instead of the grand, strong man my wife thinks me?'

The wife smiled and patted his hand.

'I know my own man! And it's not my man that would take all the world has to offer without giving anything back.'

'Flatterer!' laughed her husband, rubbing his cheek against her hair, 'I'll begin to think that Mrs McRobbie is fonder of pomp and circumstance than I'd given her credit for.'

Lizzie turned quickly and put both hands on his shoulders. Her eyes were full of tears.

'It's not that, heart's love, and well you know it! I'd as lief live back on the farm for the rest of my life if I thought you'd be happy back there too. But it's not to be. We can't escape the responsibilities of wealth, and here's the finger pointing out the way.'

'You know I'd just hate it, Liz, living in the public eye, with the searchlight turned on us all the time. And it would put an end to all the plans we've made for travelling.'

'We'd not enjoy them if we hadn't done our duty by our country first. The way is clear Carter, tho' it points uphill as far as we can see, but that's the way we must go!'

And so the appointment was confirmed.

That same morning a very different scene was being enacted over in Victoria. Mrs Morley sat at her breakfast table amusing herself with her engagement book the while she waited for her husband to join her.

She wore a negligée of pink silk and lace, with diamonds on her fingers and in her ears. Her hair was very carefully marcelled and dressed and her face was so heavily powdered that no particle of natural coloured skin was visible at all. Rose Morley, in her early days, had passed as a fine looking woman, but her expression now was such that unless she were actually smiling with pleasure (and this was a very rare occurrence with her) her face was repellent.

Impatiently she pulled her grapefruit towards her and began to eat it. The table was crowded with silver and carnations, which, however, failed to outscent Mrs Morley's powder. Presently a step on the stairs and her husband came in, closing the door and standing there at the opposite end of the table with a hand on the back of his chair.

It is doubtful whether his wife would have even looked up at his entrance if it had not been for this strange pause he made instead of drawing out his chair and sitting down in the usual way. When she did look up, she put down her spoon and stared at him in astonishment.

'Why, Gordon! Whatever is the matter with you? Are you ill? You haven't shaved and you look as if you'd been up all night anyway! Where've you been? Why didn't you tell me you weren't coming home last night?'

The man stood looking across the carnations at her, rather impersonally, as though she were one of the pieces of furniture. He was sallow from lack of sleep and the whites of his eyes were bloodshot; the lines in his face had become deep furrows, and cheeks and jowl sagged with fatigue.

'I've come to tell you —' he began, but she interrupted him.

'Have you heard who's been made Lieutenant-Governor?' she asked, with quickened interest.

'Carter McRobbie,' he replied.

'*What!*' cried Rose, clutching the table with both hands, '*me take second place to Lizzie Laidlaw*, that plain little farm-chit queening it at Government House!' Her face was becoming blotched with passion and her voice rose to the verge of hysteria.

'You knew it, Gordon, you knew it all the time, and you could have prevented it! You just knew how I'd hate it, and yet you'd let them do it. *I tell you I won't have it, I'll die first!*'

In the heat of her temper, the expression of deepening disgust on her husband's face escaped her notice. Her voice rose to a shriek.

'Well, why don't you speak? Why don't you say you'll have it altered? I'll not —'

The man broke in on the tirade.

'Stop!' he said in a low, sharp word of command, and made a gesture with his hand as though to push away her flow of talk. Strange to say she did stop; there was that in his tone that forced obedience.

'Enough of this nonsense! I've come to tell you something very much more important — *to you*. I've lost nearly every bit of my money! All that is secure is what is tied up in your name. Not only this, but circumstances have arisen which make it advisable for me to give up my position at once and leave the country. We could live in a humble way in England or in Australia, whichever you like. I give you your choice. Either stay here alone and live on what money you've got, or come with me. Which is it to be?'

The woman's face changed completely while the man spoke, the colour faded away, leaving it ashen. She let go her hold on the table and sank back limply. Twice she opened her mouth to speak, but she was trembling so that the words would not come.

The clock ticked patiently on. The man standing at the other side of the table regarded her without one trace of softening or sympathy on his face. He just stood waiting for his answer.

'Is all that true?' she whispered at last.

'Quite,' he replied shortly, 'if you are coming with me, you had better go upstairs and begin packing, we leave tomorrow morning.'

The very concrete suggestion of hurry was something definite enough for her to grasp.

'*Never!*' This time her voice was hideous with hysteria. 'If you've dragged me down to this, *you can go alone*, and I'll keep what I've got, thank you! You think you can play the fool with your own money and then live on mine, do you? Well, you're mistaken for once. You've made your own bed, go and lie on it!'

She stopped for lack of breath, and fell to sobbing noisily.

'Ah,' said Morley, 'so you're just a fair-weather friend, Rose, after all. You were willing enough to share my prosperity, but you cast me off altogether rather than share my poverty!'

'Good God!' she shrieked at him between her sobs, 'you drag me down in the dirt just now of all times when that brazen klootch Lizzie's there preening herself ready to look down on me – and not content with that you cast it up at me that I won't go with you – and live on nothing, Heaven knows where – just because I've got too much self-respect. *Oh, you brute! You brute!*' She clenched her hands together and rocked herself to and fro in an utter abandonment of fury.

The man turned away and put his hand on the door handle. He looked back at her with contempt.

'That your last decision, Rose, those your last words to me? You won't see me again!'

'*Go, I hate the sight of you!*' she shrieked at him, wringing her hands.

And Gordon Morley opened the door and went, without another word.

The woman left behind went on rocking wildly to and fro, moaning and sobbing to herself.

When the mid-day boat from Victoria landed her passengers in Vancouver, there were those who recognised the Premier as he walked up from the wharf and drove off at once in a taxi. He had no grips of any kind, so the few who remarked him concluded that he had come over on a rush visit and would return to Victoria that night.

He drove straight to Craddock Low's private house and dismissed the taxi. Before long he was talking with Mrs Low in the drawing room.

'But he's not fit to see *anyone*, Mr Morley, not even yourself, old friend that you are. Why, you don't realise how ill he is; he *wouldn't know you!*'

'Tut, tut,' said Morley, frowning and shaking his head, 'how long
has he been like this?'

'Oh, it's been coming on gradually for some time. I forget how
long it is since you've seen him. But it's reached a climax now, the
doctors see that I can't keep him at home any longer. They're going
to take him away this week!'

Mrs Low's voice broke and she felt for her handkerchief.

'What did you say the doctors call it?' asked Morley.

' "GPI" – General Paralysis of the Insane. It takes different forms
you know. He's *very* bad just now! It's a good thing we have no
white servants, they wouldn't have stayed, but Ling, our old China-
boy seems to understand him and he's the only one that can do
anything with him when he's worst!'

Even as she spoke there came strange sounds from upstairs,
moans rising in crescendo to a hoarse scream in a man's voice, then a
thud.

Mrs Low put her hand up to her face in horror. 'There he is again,
I hope Ling is with him,' and she ran from the room.

Morley followed her upstairs. Through the open door of a bed-
room he saw the man who had been known as Craddock Low, once
the most brilliant barrister in British Columbia, writhing on the floor
like a worm dropped from a spade.

Mrs Low ran to him, but as she stooped to help him up, the man
beat at her with feeble fists.

'Take care Mrs Low, keep away,' said Morley, 'he's mad, he might
hurt you!' and he also stopped to catch hold of Low by the
shoulders.

The writhing man caught at Morley's hand and looked up at him
with glazed, dilated eyes, in which the pupil was so full as to make
them look opaque, like the eyes of an Oriental. So emaciated was his
face that the skin was stretched like parchment over the bones. He
had lost control over the muscles of his mouth, which quivered and
dribbled horribly.

There was no sign of recognition in his eyes when he saw Morley,
nothing but madness.

As he clutched at the hands trying to lift him, he let forth words
which ran into one another in a moaning tone.

'Just a few grains – quick – for God's sake, *go, get it now –* I'll
give you my soul,' he went on mumbling and mouthing.

'What in Heaven's name is it that he wants?' asked Morley. But at that moment Ling, the China-boy, came into the room and said a few words in Chinese to the man on the floor. Immediately the writhing form raised itself and, twisting round, the thing that had once been Craddock Low flung itself at the Chinaman's feet with frantic arms clutching about the Chinaman's knees.

'Give it me quick or I shall die – quick!'

'Ugh!' exclaimed Morley, starting backwards, *'it's opium*, is it?'

'Hush, oh, *don't* say it outside, Mr Morley,' said Mrs Low, twisting her hands together, 'we are telling everyone it's GPI!'

Morley turned to Ling: 'Another of your victims, you rotten, yellow scum!' he said, between his teeth.

But Ling only smiled.

Chapter 18

In which we meet Chung Lee again as a winner

A MAN WAS HURRYING down Pender Street towards Chinatown at midnight. The collar of his top-coat was turned up and his soft hat was dragged well down over his eyes, but even so, as he neared the Chinese section more than one passing Chinaman signalled to his fellows by way of showing that he recognised the white man.

At a certain alley-way he stopped and looked back up the street. At the same moment two Chinamen, who had been following him half a block behind all the way from the West End, stepped aside into the shadows, but he saw them.

The alley into which he turned was dark as ink and foetid with rotting vegetables and refuse. He felt his way along the wall until he came to a door on which he tapped with his nails, three times. Evidently he was expected, for the door opened almost at once and he passed into a darkness even blacker than that outside.

A match was struck and a lantern lit, showing a passage and two Chinamen in dirty European dress, without coats on. A word or so and they guided the visitor through a room at the end of the passage in which the air was so thick and foul that he nearly choked. It was a small room of about twelve feet square and the walls were lined with bunks from floor to ceiling, each bunk containing two or more Chinamen, sleeping. There must have been between forty and fifty of them.

The floor was thick and slimy with unnameable filth of unsanitary humanity and a lazy rat loped across the room in front of the newcomers. There were no windows at all.

Through this pest-hole they passed and downstairs into a basement storeroom, where several groups of Chinamen sat gambling, down more stairs cut out of the earth itself and into a room where a dozen Chinamen, all talking at once, made a babel of sound which stopped suddenly at the entrance of the white men.

The one who appeared to be the chairman of the Orientals, sitting cross-legged on a chair at the far end of the room, was that self-same Chung Lee we saw ten years ago humbly peddling vegetables along the Point Grey road.

In the intervening years Chung Lee had waxed fat and heavy on the proceeds of innumerable deals in illicit drugs and the profits from many gambling dens.

His body was ponderous and protuberant, so that he now walked with dignity and, perforce, slowly; his face was fat and flabby with several double chins, and when he smiled his little black eyes disappeared altogether.

The door shut to and the white man stood with his back against it surveying the Orientals like a stag at bay. Then the talking began again.

After an hour the door opened once more and the white man came out in a great hurry and banged the door after him. He paused a moment to take out his handkerchief and wipe his brow; his mouth was grim, but his eyes were desperate.

Then he dashed upstairs the way he had come and out into the street again. Quickly as he hurried along, almost running, he could not escape the vigilance of the two Chinamen who had followed him before and who picked up his trail again the moment he left the alley.

On he went till he came to Columbia Street, then he turned down towards the sea. There were few people about at this time and even the wharves were deserted. The man's haste became such that his followers had to trot to keep him in sight.

The last North Vancouver ferry had long since come and gone and the night-watchman, dozing in his shanty, never saw the man who ran across the CPR tracks and onto the landing stage. There was no moon anyway, so nobody saw him or the two who followed after.

When he came up to the fence he stopped a little, breathless with his hurry, and leant upon it a moment or so. During that pause the pad-pad of running feet reached his ears and he listened till the sound suddenly stopped and then he turned his head quickly, just in time to see dimly thro' the darkness the two figures slip behind a deserted stall.

Swearing to himself, he took from his pocket an electric torch, walked back and flashed it behind the stall, but there was nobody there, and no sound at all but the hum of the traffic in the city and the dull booming wash of the sea against the wharves.

He went back to the fence and climbed up till he stood on the top of it. Then he looked back at the city again and for some vague reason took out his watch and flashed the torch on it to see the time. And the light showed up the face of Gordon Morley, Premier of BC. But there were only two who saw him.

Then he jumped. Just a splash that no one heard, and the waves went on washing against the wharf with a dull, monotonous boom.

The two Chinamen came out from their hiding-place and went their way. Their task was over.

The funeral of the Hon. Gordon Morley, Premier of BC, was as pompous and impressive as his position necessitated, but the mystery of his death remained unsolved. Some said foul play and some said suicide, but as there was no evidence to hand in support of either the inquest held after his body was found floating in the Inlet resulted in a verdict of death by misadventure.

When they broke the news to his widow they found her strangely unshocked by it; it was almost as if she had been prepared to hear something of the sort and, though she made a great show with handkerchiefs and sobs, her emotion lacked the spontaneous touch of sincerity.

She attended the funeral billowing with crepe and black jet and herself presided over a solemn reception for certain prominent mourners at her house afterwards, with utterly tearless eyes and well-powdered nose.

In all the long cortege that followed Gordon Morley to his grave, there was not one who shed a tear of regret for the man that was gone; not one who wished him back again; never a heart so full of loving memories that it took the colour from a single cheek.

And so ended the career of that most successful man – as the world counts success – Gordon Morley. Yet, as the evil that men do lives after them, so there came to light after this man's death certain stark revelations as to the deeds of his lifetime and his business connections.

One of the most startling bits of news that leaked out somehow was about Morley's purchase of the sugar refinery. It seemed that he had been nothing more nor less than a figurehead acting as paid manager for a *company of Chinese capitalists, who owned all the stock*!

This discovery so stirred and horrified the business world of Vancouver that every attempt was made to hush it up, and a collection of monied men who realised the seriousness of denationalising such an industry, banded together with an effort to buy it back again. But the Chinese flatly refused to sell – at any price.

Just about this time our friend Harding, the Fish Inspector, came on the scene again. He had, to a certain extent, gained the object for which he had been working – the reconstruction of the fishing laws of the Province so as to make it next to impossible for the Japs to gain any further hold in this industry.

But in spite of this it still seemed that the number of little brown men who went out in chug-chug boats to do their business in deep waters was on the increase, and still the law winked its eye and looked the other way.

Harding's eyes opened wide on this fact at last when a friend sought his advice as to the advisability of putting his money into a new cannery to be built on the Fraser River.

'I should have thought,' said Harding, 'that there were so many Jap canneries there already that there was no room for any new ones, especially a white one. Where, for instance, would you buy your fish?'

'From fishermen, I guess. Nationalities don't worry me any!' the friend replied.

'They will before you're through, I'm thinking,' answered Harding drily, 'but you can't be ignorant of the fact that the Japs always combine to crowd out any white fisherman who starts in round the mouth of the Fraser? And that being the case you'd be bound to buy all your fish from Japs, and they might prefer to sell to their own canneries, so it is more than possible that you'd find yourself left one day!'

'Oh, come off it, Harding, that's just what the war's done to you chaps. You can't stop pitting nation against nation and applying your doctrine to everyday life! Why on earth should fishermen refuse to sell fish to anyone who'll buy, just because they're another nationality?'

'All right,' said Harding, shortly, 'go ahead! If you like to put yourself in such a position that you're utterly dependent on Japs for the means wherewith to run your business, and dependent on the *prices they set* because they have a monopoly of the trade and no one can compete with them — very well, go right in and don't let *me* stop you! You'll come right out pretty soon, if I know anything about it, a wiser man than you went in!'

The friend departed to seek further someone who would give him such advice as he wished to hear. Harding, on the other hand, put in his time gathering together such detailed information as would lead to the prosecution of certain cannery-owners and many of their employees for illegally selling their independent licenses to Jap fishermen to be used under cover of the white man's name on the license.

When he had collected enough details to convince any disinterested person about the state of things in the fishing industry, he laid his paper before the Fisheries Board. The way it was received would have confirmed the worst suspicions of an onlooker.

'You're a fool to have meddled with it at all, Harding,' he was told, 'do you want to lose your job?'

'Of course not, but I'd rather do that than keep my mouth shut when opening it might save BC's staple industry *for BC!*'

'Take my advice and leave this alone, *forget it!* We'd all lose our jobs if this information reached the public. The fish trade has too many capitalists mixed up in it who are *dependent on yellow labour*, and the Government daren't interfere — you know that as well as I do!'

Harding stood with his back to the wall.

'If you don't take that up and prosecute publicly, in the lawful way,' he said, 'I'll take it upon myself to make the whole thing public!'

His chief laughed drily.

'I'm afraid you've struck a big snag this time, Harding! As I said before, you're a fool! And now good-day to you, I'm busy!'

Within the week Harding received a notice calling for his resignation. He lost his job. True to his word, he made every attempt to have his information made public through the press. But no newspaper would print it; the offence they might cause by so doing would lose them so many valuable advertisements that they refused to take the risk.

Harding felt himself in the position of a man driving a herd of pigs who were stubbornly heading for a precipice. The more he tried to head them off the more they ran round him, heading for their own destruction.

There was no one to whom he could turn, no one it seemed who was disinterested enough to take steps to help him. And what could one man do against the powers that be, powers that refused to see?

At this juncture there was one name that kept returning constantly to his mind, and that was the name of Mrs McRobbie, the wife of the new Lieutenant-Governor. Strange that it was herself and not her husband that he should instinctively turn to of all people, in his time of doubt and perplexity, but there it was, her personality stood out in his mind as the shadow of a great rock in a thirsty land.

Chapter 19

In which the lieutenant-governor is confronted by a choice

MRS MCROBBIE TOOK FAR more interest in politics than she did in her social duties, which latter one must acknowledge that she neglected rather scandalously. And, as he always found that her judgment was sane and far-sighted, her husband fell into the habit of discussing politics with her and came to rely more than a little upon her opinion.

Like most men whose natural instinct is honesty, McRobbie was transparent as glass to the woman who loved him, so that on the evening he came home more than common tired with the weight of many responsibilities on his shoulders, his wife listened patiently to the ostensible reasons for his weariness before she asked him the real reason.

'But there's something else weighing on your mind, Carter. What's worrying you, dearest?'

He moved uncomfortably in his chair and tried to avoid answering her, but she pressed the point.

'It's the methods of these members that worry me,' he said at last. 'They try to rush measures through in ten minutes that are important enough to require ten months of discussion.'

'And then expect you to sign them automatically, I suppose, without a wee bit of time to consider whether you'd be doing right or wrong?'

'Oh, but I'm looked upon as a mere figurehead, certainly not supposed to offer any opposition to any measure they may choose to pass!'

'Still, you must never forget you have that right, and nothing can take it from you. So it's some special measure that's fretting you tonight, something you don't like to sign?'

In spite of his cares, Carter laughed.

'You're a witch, sweetheart, or a mindreader, or both.'

Lizzie smiled and knitted on in silence waiting. But this time she waited in vain, for instead of explaining further her husband rose and paced up and down the room.

'They've *no business*,' he exclaimed hotly, 'to leave the whole responsibility of a thing like this on my shoulders! It isn't right! Why should it be left to *me* of all people to decide!'

He was speaking more to himself than to her.

This discomposure in her husband was something so unusual that Lizzie knew how serious a thing it was that was on his mind. But she knitted on placidly.

'I think it's a mighty good thing it *is* you and nobody else has to decide,' she said soothingly. 'You at any rate, have the backing of education, an honest heart and a disinterested mind.'

He stopped in his pacing and looked down at her. 'How do you make so sure that I *am* disinterested? One is only human, hang it all!'

Lizzie felt her lips go dry, but she looked up at him and smiled.

'I know you better than you know yourself, my man! It isn't in you to do downright wrong however much it would help or hurt your own affairs!'

He passed his hand wearily over his brow.

'Yet, they all seem to think it right – though I keep telling them it would be the thin end of the wedge.'

'Can't you tell me what it is?' Lizzie asked.

He stopped again and looked at her, then paced on impatiently.

'No, no, I must make my own decision this time, you are prejudiced in this matter.'

It was then that Lizzie began to suspect what the matter was, but again she held her peace.

'Well, well, come and rest! You will think more clearly in the morning. You needn't sign anything tonight surely?'

'Oh, no, they've allowed me the grace of tomorrow to think it over, thank God!'

And they went upstairs. But McRobbie had told his wife more by his actions than by his words. All she had to go upon was that his mind was in a turmoil over a certain measure that had been hurried through Parliament by Members who had been particularly anxious that they should not be given the usual opportunities for public discussion. She had never known him quite so worried before, and the very fact of his refusal to discuss the matter with her gave ground for certain fancies to formulate in her mind.

The morrow came and with it a telephone message and a visitor for the Lieutenant-Governor. He was out when the message came, but the caller asked for Mrs McRobbie. She went to the 'phone and found that the man at the other end was one Young Lung Kow, of whom she knew only as an influential Chinaman. Young Lung smiled to himself when he asked for Mrs McRobbie and gave her the message intended for her husband.

He made the mistake of judging all white women by Mrs Gordon Morley, whom he had met on occasions. With a polite request that the message be taken down on paper, word for word, it was given:

'Please inform the Lieutenant-Governor that Young Lung Kow finds himself in a position to supply His Honor with all the labor he requires in his canneries. It is for himself to decide whether he wishes *the help* of Young Lung Kow *or otherwise!*'

The last two words were repeated twice with emphasis, and Mrs McRobbie left the telephone with more than a little sense of uneasiness. She read the message over several times and became more and more impressed by the existence in it of a double meaning.

'It reads to me like a threat, Carter,' she said when she handed the message to him.

'It *is* a threat,' he replied, frowning over it.

'But why should a Chinaman threaten *you?*' she asked, grasping his arm in both her hands. 'Would it mean so much to you if you were not able to get Chinese help for your canneries?'

'It would cripple the industry so much that it would be years before it could recover, and then I could never compete with other canneries!'

It was now that Lizzie McRobbie falsified the opinion of Young Lung Kow with regard to white women.

'I would rather live on dry bread so that you might run them at a loss on white labour, than be rich and *dependent on the goodwill of a Chinaman!*'

She took his face between her hands and looked into his very soul with eyes that she had inherited from her father, but they were brimful of love.

'And you feel that way too, my man,' she went on. 'Thank God ye are too leal for a Chink to have power over ye!'

The man sighed and kissed her, and his eyes were dark with worry.

'If it were only Chinks, Lizzie – but they're all against me – I'm standing alone in this!'

'And well are ye fitted to stand alone, or they wouldn't have chosen you. But come away to dinner now, some nice hot broth will banish half the worries, I'm thinking!'

But Lizzie's heart was heavy as lead for all that her words were stout and comfortable.

Hardly had the nice hot soup disappeared and the joint taken its place, when a visitor was announced – on urgent business, and the maid who waited handed a card to the Lieutenant-Governor. He started a little, frowning at the card in his hand, and pushed back his chair impatiently.

'Excuse me, dearest, I must see what this fellow wants, I'll be back in a minute!'

'Mary, who was that man who came just now?' Mrs McRobbie asked the maid.

'He didn't give his name, Madam, he looked like a Japanese!'

Mrs McRobbie pondered uneasily over her answer. Why on earth should her husband be beset with Orientals today? The Chinaman had threatened him, was that what the Japanese had come for also? The first threat was somehow connected with the matter that was worrying him, the bill which was awaiting his signature, she guessed that much. And then a great light dawned on her. It must be that this bill concerned the Orientals – affected them vitally.

She put down her knife and fork and leant back in her chair with that creepy feeling that comes to us all when we have prescience of great danger. She rose and left the room, crossing the hall to her husband's study with no clearer purpose in mind than an instinctive desire to protect him from some danger she could not understand.

She put her hand on the doorknob, but found it held from inside. The visitor, evidently, was just about to depart, and with his hand on the handle spoke his parting words.

'Tomorrow I send message to River's Inlet, it will be either "*Come out*," or "*Stay there!*" Only *you* know which it will be!'

Lizzie moved away before she could hear her husband's answer. She felt like a spy, but she had heard enough to convince her that the purport of the Jap's errand was synonymous with the message of the Chinaman.

'Who was the visitor?' she asked McRobbie when he came back to the table.

'Hoshimura,' he answered. 'You've heard me speak of the manager of my Jap fishermen up North?'

'Yes, and the man we met as a bellboy at the Vancouver Hotel, when we were talking with Mr Harding?'

'The very same, what a memory you've got, Liz!'

She said no more just then; she saw that her husband ate scarcely anything and that his face was drawn and haggard. It was not until they were alone and sitting over the fire that she broached the subject again, and then she went straight to the point.

'Did Hoshimura come to threaten you, too, Carter?'

'It looks like it, certainly. It depends on his say-so within the next twenty-four hours whether my canneries find themselves boycotted or not by the Jap fishermen!'

'But are *all* the fishermen up there Japs?'

'The others are so few that they hardly count. Anyway the little devil knows only too well that it would bring my canneries to a standstill if I found myself unable hereafter to buy fish from his men.'

'What an awful state of things! What did you tell him?'

'Nothing at all. But he went away quicker than he came!'

Just then McRobbie was called to the telephone, and Lizzie rose and went over to draw the curtains. She was desperately uneasy, knowing that it would require all her tact, all her love and all her own strength of mind to help her husband through the stress of a terrible temptation and a vital decision.

Her hands went up to press her temples as she stared down unseeing on the litter of papers lying about the desk. But some typewritten words caught her attention.

'*Summary of Act Granting Extension of Franchise to Chinese and Japanese Land-Owners*,' she read with startled eyes that gradually realised the import of the words. Her heart almost stood still. Instinctively she knew that this was the "measure" that was the cause of all his worry, that had been rushed through without public discussion by Members who had 'axes to grind' — the measure that would become law on the signature of the Lieutenant-Governor. Small wonder that he had spoken of it as the 'thin end of the wedge'!

All her father's prophecies anent the sale of the country to the Asiatics came crowding back to her mind. And now the man she loved was standing with his back to the wall, fighting for the future of his country against the urge of his self-seeking fellows and the threats of Orientals.

Being a woman she knew that her power over him was such that she could influence him against all the powers in the world if need be, but she also knew that he would stand strong forever in her estimation (and still more important – in his own) if he won the fight alone.

So McRobbie found her knitting peacefully in the big arm-chair opposite his own when he came back and flung himself into it exhausted, like a man far spent.

'Come over and kiss me, Liz,' he said at last.

She went over and sat on the arm of his chair, holding his head to her with her cheek against his forehead.

'I don't know what I should do without you, Liz!' The tears were in her eyes as she suppressed the desire that every woman has at times to treat her man as though he were her baby. But it was no time for that.

'Ye'll never stop flattering me, Carter – trying to make me believe you're no dependent on yourself! You, the wise, strong man on whom all the country is depending this very day. What a mercy they chose you, sweetheart, instead of some weakling who would never hesitate to give in to the worst of them if so it might serve his own interests!'

The man moved uneasily; he lifted his wife's hand and kissed it, but he said nothing, just stared into the fire. They sat on in silence for several minutes and then the fire fell in with a crash and Lizzie got up to mend it. Then she went back to her own chair and took up her knitting again.

'D'ye mind that quotation from Shakespeare, Carter, that Dad was so fond of? *"To thine own self be true. And it must follow as the night the day, thou cans't not then be false to any man!"* '

He tried to remember when and where he had heard those words before, they brought back a flood of memories from the past – a class-room in that ancient school overseas where his father had sent him to learn tradition; rows of desks in an oak-panelled room with the sunlight from a high window making patterns on the floor;

sleepy boys longing to be outside with the drone of the bees and the scent of Madonna lilies on the hot summer's afternoon; the patient voice of the classical master as he rolled off the sonorous, grand old Latin words of an age-old poet and expounded their meaning.

The boys, indifferent though they appeared to his teaching at the time, had loved that master. He was old and white-haired, a scholar and a gentleman. McRobbie remembered, as it were yesterday, that last lesson he gave them at the end of the term when he retired.

Some boy had chalked up on the blackboard Kipling's words —

Let us now praise famous men
  Men of little showing,
For their work lives after them...
  Greater than their knowing.

He remembered how the old man had stood reading the words with his back to the boys for a long, long time, and when he turned to begin the lesson there had been a break in his voice.

How they had cheered him at the end — boisterously to hide any emotion, as boys will, and then his parting words — 'Boys, I hope when we meet again, as we undoubtedly will, in this world or the next, that I may be able to say of each one of you how proud I am to have helped a little in the forming of your characters! Play your parts in life as you would play one of your school games — honestly, fearlessly, *cleanly, for the good of your country and not for yourselves!*

Never let any man coerce you into doing a thing which you cannot look back on with a free and easy conscience. *Fear God! Love the brotherhood! Honor the King!*'

Part 3

The future

Chapter 20

In which positions are reversed

CARTER MCROBBIE and a friend stood looking on at the wholesale lumber operations going on in Stanley Park. The park had been sold by the city a short time back to a company of Chinamen who had already felled all the big timber and were busy hauling it off to mills on False Creek; there were only four mills in Vancouver now that did not belong to them, and these were owned by Japs.

The two white men who stood gazing helplessly at this utter destruction of what had once been the pride of BC, cursed below their breath and gnashed their teeth as they discussed it. The sale should never have been permitted, said one, but then, asked another – who was to stop it? The mayor and all the aldermen except two were Chinamen!

And as they stood there, a big touring car came whizzing round the bend heading straight for the group and making no sort of attempt to avoid them. They leapt out of the way but one was not agile enough and the corner of the car knocked him flat down onto the road. The man sitting beside the chauffeur in the car leant out and swore smoothly and scornfully at his poor fool of a victim who had dared to stand in his way and obstruct his passage, and then he drove on. McRobbie recognized him as Young Lung Kow.

The man was badly hurt. The others made a stretcher of their arms and started out for the nearest house. But they had to carry him a long way; nearly all the houses in the West End belonged to Chinamen and very few white people lived there now. None of these men owned motor-cars, they had sold them long ago because gasoline, which had been cornered by the Chinese, was so prohibitive a price that no whites could afford it.

There was no hope whatever of getting redress for the 'accident,' deliberate as it had been, because all the policemen were Chinese and waxed peculiarly offensive and even dangerous when approached by a white man with a case against their own countrymen.

The drains were up in the street down which they passed, and the road all in disorder. Down in the trench were white men at regular intervals, working for dear life with pick and shovel, while along each side of it walked two Chinamen, the foremen, who saw to it that there was no sort of slackening in the work of the men under their charge.

They came at last to a house where still a white man lived. In the garden next door the Chinese mistress of the house was taking much interest in the making of a lawn; she was directing – with unintelligible shrieks and gesticulations – the movements of a burly man with a hod and shovel whom McRobbie recognized as one, Thompson, erstwhile Customs Officer at Victoria.

They phoned for a doctor, but all the doctors were busy fighting the plague of typhoid fever that was rampant all over the land; however, McRobbie volunteered to go out and trace one from the last house of call, so off he went.

He was lucky enough to come up with one he knew hurrying along in an antiquated horse and rig so he got in and drove back with him.

'It's getting worse, McRobbie,' the doctor said with a worried look, 'and we are just powerless to stop it! There aren't nearly enough of us to cope with it, the hospitals are too full already, we've turned all the schools into hospitals, and fresh cases are reported every day! And as for nurses – well, they are not to be had for love or money!'

'I know that,' put in McRobbie, 'my wife is hardly ever at home now, she spends all her time nursing round the neighbourhood! If only we could trace the source of it? Have you no suspicion as to what it's caused by?'

'Yes, I have,' replied the doctor, shortly, 'and if my suspicions are correct, there's nothing to be done except for us all to clear out of this country as soon as possible!'

'What do you mean?'

'Well, it seems a curious thing, doesn't it, that this epidemic should be carrying off the white people like flies while there are so few, if any, cases among the Orientals? Of course the Chinese have their own doctors and hospitals and so have the Japs, but I'll swear that only one per cent of the cases in them now are typhus! But we all know that the Asiatics are peculiarly immune to this particular disease, innured to it by countless generations of living without sanitation!'

'Good heavens, Doc! Then what do you suspect? I wouldn't put anything past the brutes!'

'I'm carrying out an exhaustive analysis of all foods. I will let you know the result in a few days' time. But even if what I suspect is true, we can do *nothing!* Absolutely *nothing*, except, as I said before, to clear out of the country!'

McRobbie left the doctor setting the broken leg of the man who had been knocked down, and with one of the others went on his way down to the town. And as they went, they discussed the plausibility of the doctor's suspicions.

'Come to think of it, what foods coming into the city are there that do *not* pass thro' Chinese hands?'

'That's right! They own the stock of every canned milk factory in town, they own the sugar refinery, every vegetable bought in Vancouver is grown by them, and I hear that they have more than a little interest in this big new meat combine that's just been formed!'

'Yes, and there are mighty few groceries now that are owned by white men! They seem to be divided up between the Chinks and the Japs. Of course the Japs have shipping enough to get their own exclusive supplies in from outside without dealing with the Chinks – they get their sugar straight from Honolulu for instance. As for fish – well the Minister of Marine and Fisheries being a Jap, no white man is even allowed a license and whenever we try to buy any they just put the prices up sky-high!'

'Did you see who that was in the car that knocked down poor old Bates?'

'Some damned yellow devil; did you know him?'

'Yes, I knew him. It was Young Lung Kow, the Attorney-General!'

'Good God! What a state of things! What condemned forsaken fools we were to give our support to the agitators at Ottawa who allowed Canada to secede from the Empire! We've no one to look to for help, *no one to back us* – and we've failed all along the line!'

'What will be the end of it all?' said McRobbie, more to himself than the other.

'What was the *beginning of it all?*' cried the other. 'Look back and see! Wasn't it during your Governorship, McRobbie, that they passed that law extending the franchise to Oriental land-owners? See what it has led to!'

McRobbie put his arm up as tho' to ward off a blow and reeled back against the wall like a drunken man.

'*Don't!*' he gasped in a broken voice, '*God forgive me for signing that!* They all brought pressure to bear on me, and I didn't realise — how could I foresee what would happen?'

'Oh, come on, come on!' said the other impatiently, 'what's done can't be undone now! I guess you weren't to blame any more than the rest of us anyway, *I* was one of the Members who advocated that Act if you want to know! But *I had to*, I had all my money in a concern that was dependent on cheap labor — yellow labor — and the Chinks brought pressure on me too!'

They walked silently on into Granville Street, two shamed men, self-condemned and suffering.

Granville Street was crowded. But there were few white men to be seen, and those were hustled and jostled as they attempted to make their way through the busy streams of Orientals. All the stores on either side bore the names of Chinese or Japanese owners, and all were prosperous and full of trade. Inside them white men and women served behind the counters and ran to do the bidding of imperious Chinese women who came to do their morning's shopping.

The two men made their way up to the Hotel Vancouver. The CPR was now owned by a company of Chinamen and the manager of the hotel was one Chung Lee, once a vegetable vendor.

McRobbie recognised a friend he had known as a big timber-merchant in better days, who was occupied with a carpet-sweeper in the saloon, sweeping up cigar ash from round the feet of a fat Chinaman who persistently flicked his ash onto the floor. Work was so scarce for white men in these days that any who had not money enough to get out of the country were forced to take what they could get.

McRobbie went up to the sweeper and asked him if lunch was over and if they could get anything to eat. The man shook his head doubtfully, but 'Come along,' he said, 'we'll go to the head waiter, if he's in a good temper he may fix you up!'

McRobbie recognised the head waiter as Sing Wo, a servile, ob-sequious man who had once been in his employ as head of the Chinese packers in his biggest cannery. But Sing had had his orders anent the serving of meals after regular hours to white folk. He merely sneered at the request.

'You go buyum Hotel youself, Mac, then bymbye you eatee all-same you like! I won't tink, eh!'

McRobbie started forward with his fist raised, his temper up.

'*How dare you speak to me like that, you scum!*'

'*Take care, take care,* McRobbie,' warned the other white man, coming forward quickly. But Sing Wo showed no discomposure. He clapped his hands and called out a few words to the waiters in the dining-room. Immediately he was surrounded by twenty or more Chinamen ready waiting to do his bidding.

A few words from him and they laid hands on McRobbie and the man with him ran them forcibly out of the hotel and flung them roughly down the steps and onto the sidewalk below.

When Carter McRobbie had retired from the Governorship, they had sold the house in Victoria; Lizzie had never been really happy there and always pined for the farm. So they had come back to live on Lulu Island.

When McRobbie reached home that night, even more bruised in spirit than he was in limb after the disgraceful fracas at the hotel, he was perturbed to find the house in gloom and his wife lying on a sofa with her face to the wall.

'*My sweetheart! what is the matter?* Aren't you well, dearest?' he cried out, dropping down on his knees beside her.

She turned a flushed face and looked at him wearily.

'I shall be all right, dear, don't worry! I'm so tired, I want to rest!'

'But how long have you felt ill, my treasure?' kissing her with an agony of fear in his heart.

'Oh, for several days, but this afternoon I just felt I *couldn't* go on nursing, so I came home!'

He got up and began to bustle about lighting a fire and a lamp.

'I'll beat up an egg in warm milk for you,' he said soothingly, 'you see you'll feel better then!' But his hands trembled and a great terror shook him as with an ague.

No amount of persuasion, however, could force Lizzie to take anything, and it was only with difficulty that Carter could persuade her to let him lift her to bed.

In vain he telephoned for a doctor. All were worked to death and even had they been free, they had no means of coming so far at that time of night. In the morning she was worse. He could get no woman to come, so he nursed her himself with the utmost care and tenderness — better than any woman — obeying to the letter orders that were 'phoned to him by the doctors who had no time to come.

But she sank fast. It was typhoid in its most virulent form. In a few days time Dr Hodges came out from town, the doctor who had come to the rescue on the day of the motor accident.

'My suspicions were correct, after all, McRobbie,' he said directly he came in, 'we have those yellow devils to thank for all this, and we had better lose no time in getting out of the country!'

'Do you mean to tell me that they've deliberately organised the spread of this plague? But how?'

'Beyond all doubt they have! I and one or two others made a pretty complete analysis of all foods, and we found that 90 per cent of all vegetables contained typhoid germs, the ones that are boiled of course stand a good chance of being rendered harmless, but only too many are eaten raw, salads and so on; 40 per cent of the canned milk in tins of a certain brand, and with the sugar we found that packages done up in blue paper were perfectly free, but those in red paper invariably contained cultures of germs — *but steady on, man!* There, sit down, you're just worn out with nursing and anxiety!

Carter had turned sick and faint with the added horror of the doctor's news. The other helped him to a chair by the open door. It was the very self-same spot where he had sat that night so long ago and listened to old Robert Laidlaw's prophecies of the future. How more than terribly true had been those prophecies, and how he, Carter McRobbie, had helped to fulfil them! Now he was reaping in full; the thing he loved more than all the world was stricken.

'I haven't slept for three days and four nights,' he told the doctor, 'my only fear is that I won't be able to keep myself awake when she wants anything!'

The doctor went in to see her. Carter scanned his face anxiously when he came out — and read the worst.

'Don't say —'

'I won't say anything, old chap, till the crisis is over! She has a grand constitution and may win through yet. But you must have help, you can't stand the strain. I'll do my best to send you a nurse this evening, meanwhile —' and here followed detailed orders.

But no nurse came. The long night hours stretched themselves out into an eternity. Lizzie, in her delirium, seemed to gather strength, so that it was all that her husband could do to hold her still. She raved and sang and shouted through that silent house and then, all at once, an hour or two after midnight, her brain cleared.

She tried to sit up, and when he gently pushed her back again, pointed an accusing finger at him.

'Don't touch me, Carter McRobbie, I despise you with all my heart for the contemptible traitor you are! I heard what the doctor said about the Chinese fouling all our food with typhoid germs! Don't you realise that it's all *your fault?* It was *you* and no one else who with your signature turned into law the Act that you *knew to be the thin end of the wedge!* It was *you who sold your country to benefit yourself, Judas that you are!* God may forgive you, but *Dad and I never will!*'

She shut her eyes and turned her face from him; he spoke to her frantically again and again, but she made never a sign.

When the chill rays of dawn stole through the curtains they saw a dead woman and a man lying on the floor beside the bed, unconscious.

Chapter 21

In which yellow wins

THE CHINESE WERE UNEASY, there was no doubt about that. They stood massed together at street corners, leaving their work and filling the air with their sing-song gabble, talking and arguing and conferring together in little knots and crowds that swelled every minute. Curious to say, there was not a Jap to be seen.

There were only a handful of white passengers that stepped off the CPR 'Limited' that morning and of them all only one, J.B. Harding, who was returning from the East, guessed the reason for all this obvious unrest. He wondered with a sinking heart, whether he had been in time with his mission.

Granville Street presented an unusual aspect as he walked up it to the Club which a few white men had managed to keep for their own exclusive use. There was scarcely any traffic, the street on either side was lined with Chinese all talking and chattering excitedly, while some were running up and down from group to group.

At the door of the club he paused and looked up the street. A white man was coming towards him, hatless, wild-eyed, dishevelled; Harding recognised him as Carter McRobbie.

'My wife is dead!' McRobbie said to him as soon as he was within speaking distance, '*They* killed her! I'm out to kill *them* now' – and he touched his pocket significantly – 'as many as I can before they get me! – Oh, no, Harding, I'm not mad, I'm sane at last!'

'Come in here, man,' replied Harding, taking the other by the arm and forcing him in at the door, 'you'll find you'll have plenty of opportunity for killing after you've listened to what I've got to tell you!'

McRobbie allowed himself to be led upstairs and into a room where there were about a dozen other men all apparently waiting for Harding. The door was immediately locked behind the two; the feeling of suppressed uneasiness and excitement amongst them was such that no one noticed trivialities like McRobbie's condition.

'I'm desperately afraid I'm too late,' Harding began. 'I think – I'm pretty certain the Japs are going to spring it on us even sooner than we expected! The Chinese know it, too. Look what the town's like this morning! The Alberta Government are sending as large an armed force as they can muster through the Rockies in motor-trucks – as we don't want any fuss with the Chinese about using the railways for this. I've warned the States and they are ready with Army and Navy to do all they can.

'But gentlemen, as I tell you, I'm afraid it's *too late* and the only way in which we can save our fellows from *utter destruction* is to organize *now*, right here, some scheme whereby we can go out and warn every white man, woman and child to *leave the country without delay*, by *any* means they can find!'

'What on earth is all this about?' questioned McRobbie, coming forward. 'I don't understand what you're all talking about!'

'Put shortly, it's this. For a long time now the Japs have been smouldering with anger against the Chinese who they think have got too great a hold in this country that they, the Japs, have always wanted for themselves. So they have been planning a gigantic raid whereby they will annihilate the Chinese and get control of the country for themselves. We got wind of it, but we kept it secret because we thought something might still be done to forestall it!'

'Good Heavens above! But what part were the white poeple in BC to play in this? What were the Japs planning to do with them?'

'Oh, no one takes any notice of the Columbians now we've dropped the British,' said Harding, bitterly. 'We are too unimportant to be considered by anybody, least of all Japs or Chinese. We're too weak to matter anyway, we'd just be annihilated along with the Chinese and those that happened to survive would be used as slaves afterwards!'

And even as he spoke a man raised his head to listen and said: *'What's that noise?'*

There was no mistaking the sound that grew louder and louder; it was that same sinister sound that had driven many out of their minds when the Germans raided England – the droning buzz of an aeroplane, *of a fleet of aeroplanes!*

Before they could get to the window, some large spherical body fell past it and landed with a dull and monstrous thud on the street below. There was an explosion that shook the floor they stood on. They looked through the window to see the shattered fragments which smoked a little, otherwise there seemed to be no damage done.

A crowd, chiefly of Chinamen, ran up to examine it, but each man, as he came within a certain distance of the thing, crumpled up and fell where he ran, like a paper doll blown over by a puff of wind. Presently there were piled heaps of men lying dead one atop of another there round the shattered shell.

'*Poison gas!*' shouted Harding. 'They're on us! Come on, men, we may be able to save some of our own kind!'

He rushed out and down stairs, closely followed by McRobbie and others. And all the time they heard other dull, terrifying explosions of the same sort, some close, some distant.

The street was a hideous chaos of death and disaster; the living ones, who ran about among piles of corpses in an attempt to find their friends, wailed and shouted in a frenzy of despair and disorder.

The aeroplanes had put out to sea again. Harding and his followers were presently joined by other white men and women, all piteously anxious to help their own kind, but as they worked among the piles of bodies and at times dragged a white one from beneath half a dozen yellow ones, in a vain hope of saving life, they realised at last that the poison-gas shells had done their work completely and instantaneously.

Harding rushed down a side street to the telephone office. A terror-stricken white girl crawled out from a booth and whimpered at him.

'*Get me Seattle,* quick as ever you can!' he shouted. But the girl only cried hysterically and it was some time before he quieted her enough to do what he wished. And then she called in vain.

'I think the wires must be down,' she said at last.

'Try Calgary then!' he urged.

But she had no more success; the wires appeared to be down in that direction also. He tried the telegraph office, but was met at the door by a frantic operator running out to tell the news that all the lines connecting Vancouver had been cut.

'So we are too late,' Harding told him grimly. 'I can do nothing, nobody can do anything! It's each for himself now, God help us all!'

It was Harding who had first got wind of the decisive intention of the Japs to come over and turn the Chinese once and forever out of BC – or 'Columbia' – as it was now called since the new regime of independence.

The latter race had gone ahead beyond all reason in a country that the Japs considered best suited to themselves. They both ignored the white man altogether. The Chinese had used him for their own purposes if he cared to stay in the country; the Japs would do the same, unless he was killed off in the general slaughter.

A conclave of whites had sent Harding as their emissary to the Republican government at Ottawa to demand protection. The reply was hardly satisfactory; 'Columbia' was autonomous and therefore if she had wanted defences, she should have provided them herself and must not look elsewhere for help; in any case, the republic had no navy or airforce and only a nominal army (as the Senate disapproved of war and armaments), so no help would be forthcoming from that direction. Certainly no part of the new Republic of Canada could ask or expect help from her erstwhile Mother — England.

The best he had been able to do was a promise of all possible help from Alberta. With the States it was another matter. Chiefly on the strength of Harding's information, they had had preparations made in apprehension of this day for a long time. Half their navy was at San Francisco and Seattle; a goodly few regiments were stationed in Washington, ready for instant service on the coast.

The Monroe Doctrine, their natural desire to protect their own race quite apart from the inadvisability of allowing the Japs such a definite hold on their own continent, were good and sufficient reasons for the stand they were ready to take.

But, as it turned out, the Japanese had double-crossed everybody, even the Chinese. Long before anyone knew that they had left Japan several squadrons bearing a flag with a Rising Sun safely stowed away in their lockers, had sailed across to the Queen Charlotte Islands, the whole southern portion of which belonged to them, and had anchored there for a week during which time the component parts of aeroplanes were pieced together and tested on the long stretches of sand that seemed intended by Nature for the purpose.

At the appointed time the battleships sailed south until they reached the north end of Vancouver Island, when they divided into two, one half sailing down the east coast, the other down the west coast, while the aeroplanes went ahead of them — with what effect we have already seen.

So perfect were the pre-concerted plans of the Japs, that several hours before the planes were sighted by any telegraph station, all communication lines were cut in the various parts of the country and 'Columbia' was completely cut off from the rest of the world.

The train by which Harding had arrived was the last to come through the CPR main line; the Connaught Tunnel was blocked up and the rails each side of it so wrecked that a fortnight's work would scarcely have righted them. Also the telegraph lines were cut. Japs from Prince Rupert saw to it that exactly the same thing was done to the GTP lines outside Fort George in the north.

The CNR lines south from Edmonton were similarly treated and the CPR southern lines through the Crow's Nest Pass. The road through the Rockies was made impassable and, lo! by the lie of the land, 'Columbia' was cut off from the West as entirely as if she was separated by an ocean.

Within the self-same hour, the Japs, who swarmed like bees in a hive along the west coast of Vancouver Island, overcame by sheer force of numbers the operators in the cable and wireless stations at Alberni, Banfield, Pachena Point and Victoria, and sent their own messages to the outside world — pleasant little messages in which was no sort of mention of Japs and the cataclysmal disturbances in 'Columbia.'

Aeroplanes dropped bombs in Victoria and Nanaimo at precisely the same minute that they were dropped in Vancouver. Later on, the American ships, steaming north out of Seattle to the rescue, found themselves hemmed in between Fort Townsend and Fort Casey by a ring of Jap ships and the rest of the American fleet coming north at full speed from San Francisco found a line of Jap ships confronting them from Cape Flattery, stretching far out into the Pacific.

The brigades of the American army marched in all haste across the border and encountered no resistance at all until they reached the Fraser when they were pulled up short. *There was no way across the river!* Both the bridges at New Westminster and at Mission had been cut.

While their engineers were finding a way out of the difficulty, they remained a target for the deadly range of Japanese guns stationed on the heights opposite them, hundreds of feet up above the river levels on the north shore. In vain their big guns were fired back; for years the Japs had been entrenching themselves against all possible attack on these heights right along the river.

Chapter 22

In which many things are made clear

CARTER MCROBBIE LAY fully twenty minutes against the wall where he had been flung by the force of the explosion before he made any attempt to move. He felt dazed, shattered and bruised all over; his right arm, on which he had fallen, was bent under him and appeared to be dislocated; it was numb and useless.

He had been standing on the wharf below the post office with Harding and they had seen with their own eyes the long, grey, terrible shapes of the Japanese war-ships as they stole through the Narrows with their deadly guns trained onto the city. The first shot had smashed up the post office with a thundering roar, the second and third, falling farther afield had sounded equally damaging; then there had been a lull, broken by the smothered shrieks of those buried under the fallen masonry, the frantic shrieks of the Chinese and the oaths and groans of white men and women.

With a great effort McRobbie pulled himself together and went off to try and do his duty by the suffering. Harding was nowhere to be seen.

He climbed with uncertain footsteps over the mountains of stone and rubble that blocked Granville Street; he slipped on something and came down with his weight on his unhurt arm, he found that his hand was resting in a pool of warm, wet blood. He looked straight into the slanting eyes of a face wedged between two blocks of stone; it was the head of a Chinaman — without a body!

Sick unto death, McRobbie got up and ran stumbling from the place, his hands dripping with blood. He ran and ran, he knew not whither, and cared not whence, so his eyes could forget the sights he had seen and his ears forget the screams.

Presently he came to an open grassy space of velvet lawns and here he flung himself down, exhausted, and let his eyes drink in the pure, healing greenness of the grass. He was on the lawns in front of the court house on Georgia Street.

How long he lay thus he could not tell, but all at once he heard his name called out in a loud voice and looked up. There on the steps of the court house stood a figure, tall, straight, clothed in nebulous grey that clung to its sides, and the face was the face of Gordon Morley, long-dead Premier of BC. And as he looked the figure raised its hand and spoke:

'*It was I* and such as I, who sold my country into the hands of aliens so that profits might accure to my own pockets! It was you, Carter McRobbie, and such as you, who ratified that sale, because you were afraid to stand alone!

'There is no forgiveness, nor is there rest for such as we. We must stay and watch the fruit of our deeds and suffer!'

'Is there nothing we can do?' cried out McRobbie. 'Is it too late?'

'There is nothing we can do,' came the answer, 'we meddled with Nature in our attempt to mix East with West and Nature is revolting at last! Carter McRobbie, you have still some years of life to live on earth, take care that in that short time you do good deeds rather than ill ones!

'All the fifty-five years of my life on earth are written on soiled and smirched pages covered with the foul record of my deeds. And for every deed I did, there opposite are written the names of the persons who suffered by it, and the higher I rose to power, the more names are written. In all those pages are only two clean ones, the one records my love for my son and the other my refusal to do the bidding of Young Lung Kow!'

'And what was that?' questioned McRobbie.

'He and his associates had bought the sugar refinery in my name, this you know. I was in their power, their net had been closing in round me for years – this through my own avarice and greed. They ordered me to pollute certain of the sugar sold to white people with a carefully prepared culture of typhoid germs, and I refused to do it! They threatened me with death, and I took my own life rather than submit to their hellish commands!'

'Is there never to be any rest for you, Gordon Morley?'

'Not until by much suffering I have developed a new soul,' the figure answered, 'for I lost the one I was born with when I was on earth. *What profiteth it a man if he gain the whole world and lose his own soul?* The tears of all those I wronged sting my heart like drops of burning blood; the cries of those on whom I trampled on my way to Wealth and Power fill my ears through all eternity, and my eyes are forced to see nothing but the fruit of all my misdeeds!'

The deafening crash of another explosion filled the air and McRobbie turned his head to listen. When he looked again, the figure had gone. He roused himself and stood up with intent to find Harding again – to be of some use still in the scheme of things, to sacrifice himself while yet there was time, to those who suffered.

When the second crash came he found himself under the Birks Building, and, looking upwards, he saw to his horror that the great pile was rocking on its base. Fascinated, he watched it leaning further and further over between him and the sky and then –

'Darling heart, wake up! Such a horrid nightmare you've been having!'

Carter McRobbie opened his eyes on the well-loved face of his wife and felt her soft arms around him.

'*Liz! Are you better?*' he gasped, unbelieving, and then, 'Where am I?' with puzzled eyes roaming round the room.

'You've been dreaming, dear, what was it all about? You've slept quite a long time and I woke you up because you were calling out so!'

He sat bolt upright and stared at her.

'Do you mean to say that was all a *dream?* Then I – there's yet time – and I *didn't* sign that bill – *thank God! Oh, thank God!*'

He rose and made a dash for the writing table, picked up the paper that had stirred Lizzie so deeply earlier in the evening, tore it up into little pieces and flung them into the fire.

Lizzie watched him, sitting still on the arm of his chair, her eyes full of thankful tears.

'Liz, *was it a dream*, or did I have a glimpse into the future? Only God knows. I only know that it has saved me and perhaps helped to save the country also! Thank high Heaven I didn't sign it! I could never have looked *you* in the face again, my dear, my dear!'

He dropped on his knees beside her and buried his face in her lap. She stroked his head tenderly, her tears rolling down her cheeks and falling onto his hair.

'Of course you didn't, sweetheart, you haven't the faith in yourself that I have! You *couldn't* and no one could force you to do a thing like that, a thing you saw was clearly wrong!'

They both forgot that she was not supposed to know anything about the matter at all.

'And now come and eat up these sandwiches, dearie,' she went on. 'I fetched them for you while you slept. You ate hardly any dinner at all!'

The man who woke up was a very different man from the one who went to sleep. The world noticed it later, but his wife knew it that evening, when he stood before her on the hearth with a new strength about him, a fresh vigour in his movements.

'Liz, I'll save the country yet, if it costs me all the wealth I've got and if we have to fight these self-seeking parasites to the death! I must get some good, clean, honourable men around me to help. Where's that fellow, Harding, I wonder? I'd like to make him my secretary.'

'How funny,' said his wife. 'He was the very man *I* had in mind too!'

'He was very vivid in my dream. I wonder –' he said slowly, 'whether it *was a dream* – or *a warning* – to tell me I was being weighed in the balance and found –'

But his wife put her hand over his mouth with a smile.

'Faithful, my man,' she finished for him. 'Faithful, as I knew you were and always will be!'

Finis

'And this is the writing that was written:

MENE, MENE, TEKEL, UPHARSIN

This is the interpretation of the thing.

MENE: God hath numbered thy kingdom and finished it.

TEKEL: Thou art weighed in the balances, and art found wanting.

PERES: Thy kingdom is divided, and given to the Medes and Persians.'